BrightRED Study Guide

Curriculum for Excellence

N5

SPANISH

Jimena Baraínca Carrión

BrightRED
PUBLISHING

First published in 2015 by:
Bright Red Publishing Ltd
1 Torphichen Street
Edinburgh
EH3 8HX

Reprinted with corrections in 2016 and 2017

A CIP record for this book is available from the British Library

ISBN 978-1-906736-56-9

With thanks to:
PDQ Digital Media Solutions Ltd (layout) and Teresa Alvarez (copy-edit)

Cover design and series book design by Caleb Rutherford – e i d e t i c

Acknowledgements
Every effort has been made to seek all copyright holders. If any have been overlooked, then Bright Red Publishing will be delighted to make the necessary arrangements.

Permission has been sought from all relevant copyright holders and Bright Red Publishing are grateful for the use of the following:
Andresr/Shutterstock.com (p 7); Monkey Business Images/Shutterstock.com (p 9); mandygodbehear/iStock.com (p 11); shvili/iStock.com (p 12); grafvision/Shutterstock.com (p 14); photomak/Shutterstock.com (p 14); Sintez/iStock.com (p 15); fotyma/iStock.com (p 16); Sam Howzit (CC BY 2.0)[1] (p 17); Caleb Rutherford e i d e t i c (pp 18-19); Carissa Rogers (CC BY 2.0)[1] (p 20); Yuri/iStock.com (p 21); S.Pytel/Shutterstock.com (p 22); Monkey Business Images/Shutterstock.com (p 23); Dennis Sabo/Shutterstock.com (p 24); 123foto/iStock.com (p 25); Alamy (p 25); Africa Studio/Shutterstock.com (p 26); BaLL LunLa/Shutterstock.com (p 30); Aleksandr Bryliaev/Shutterstock.com (p 32); haider/Shutterstock.com (p 32); iQoncept/Shutterstock.com (p 32); ollyy/Shutterstock.com (p 32); conrado/Shutterstock.com (p 32); Miguel A/Shutterstock.com (p 32); Lario Tus/Shutterstock.com (p 33); Countdown Studio (public domain) (p 33); Oleg Zabielin/Shutterstock.com (p 33); Barnaby Chambers/Shutterstock.com (p 33); Jetrel/Shutterstock.com (p 33); ventdusud/Shutterstock.com (p 33); Sergey Nivens/Shutterstock.com (p 33); Lisa F. Young/Shutterstock.com (p 33); Lorelyn Medina/Shutterstock.com (p 33); iQoncept/Shutterstock.com (p 33); Sam72/Shutterstock.com (p 33); saswell/Shutterstock.com (p 33); Martin Dougiamas (CC BY 2.0)[1] (p 32); AllanArmstrong/iStock.com (p 32); BonD80/Shutterstock.com (p 34); Rocksuzi/Dreamstime.com (p 35); Aleksandr Bryliaev/Shutterstock.com (p 36); s96serg/iStock.com (p 37); hjalmeida/iStock.com (p 38); Kolobsek/freeimages.com (p 40); Makhnach_S/Shutterstock.com (p 40); Kurt Bauschardt (CC BY-SA 2.0)[2] (p 41); Dchauy/Shutterstock.com (p 41); Roberto Caucino/Shutterstock.com (p 41); Dirima /iStock.com (p 42); ivosar/iStock.com (p 43); Christopher Lofthouse (p 41); Liudmila Gridina/Shutterstock.com (p 41); hroe/iStock.com (p 41); Greenpeace China (CC BY 2.0)[1] (p 41); michaeljung/iStock.com (p 50); Brian A Jackson/Shutterstock.com (p 51); diego_cervo/iStock.com (p 52); fotek/iStock.com (p 53); tadija/iStock.com (p 54); shironosov/iStock.com (p 55); Rawpixel/iStock.com (p 60); michaeljung/iStock.com (p 60); sasha dunaevski/freeimages.com (p 61); CandyBox Images/Shutterstock.com (p 62); Beth (CC BY 2.0)[1] (p 63); U.S. Department of Agriculture (CC BY-ND 2.0)[3] (p 63); stockyimages/iStock.com (p 64); Sergey Nivens/Shutterstock.com (p 65); © Romangorielov/Dreamstime.com (p 66); OJO_Images/iStock.com (p 67); gpointstudio/Shutterstock.com (p 70); Monkey Business Images/Shutterstock.com (p 71); FuatKose/iStock.com (p 73); Marcel Mooij/Shutterstock.com (p 74); Nykonchuk Oleksii/Shutterstock.com (p 75); bogdanhoda/Shutterstock.com (p 75); yongyuan/iStock.com (p 76); Sergey Nivens/Shutterstock.com (p 80); auremar/Shutterstock.com (p 81); Qwasyx/iStock.com (p 85); andreusK/iStock.com (p 86); petrograd99/iStock.com (p 87); wavebreakmedia/Shutterstock.com (p 90).

(CC BY 2.0)[1]   http://creativecommons.org/licenses/by/2.0/
(CC BY-SA 2.0)[2]   http://creativecommons.org/licenses/by-sa/2.0/
(CC BY-ND 2.0)[3]   http://creativecommons.org/licenses/by-nd/2.0/

Printed and bound in the UK.

CONTENTS

BRIGHTRED STUDY GUIDE: NATIONAL 5 SPANISH

SOCIETY

LEARNING

EMPLOYABILITY

CULTURE

COURSE ASSESSMENT: WRITING

COURSE ASSESSMENT

GLOSSARY

BRIGHTRED STUDY GUIDE: NATIONAL 5 SPANISH

INTRODUCING NATIONAL 5 SPANISH

During this course, you will further develop your linguistic knowledge and apply skills for learning, for life and for work purposes.

Learning any language will help you to develop your communication skills and improve your cultural knowledge about other countries.

ONLINE

The SQA website gives more detail on the grammar and suggested topics that you should know about. Follow the link from www.brightredbooks.net/N5Spanish

ONLINE

This book is supported by the BrightRED Digital Zone. Log in at www.brightredbooks.net/N5Spanish to unlock a world of videos, links, tests and much more!

THE NATIONAL 5 SPANISH COURSE

National 5 Spanish encourages you to become a more confident learner; a responsible citizen with an informed and ethical view of other cultures and traditions in Spanish-speaking countries; someone who can work independently as well as participate in group discussions and team work.

COURSE ASSESSMENT

The course assessment at National 5 has five components as outlined in the table below.

Component	Mark	Scaled Mark	Duration
Component 1: question paper 1 Listening	30	30	1 Hour and 30 minutes (for paper 1 – Reading and Writing)
Component 2: question paper 1 Writing	20	15	See above
Component 3: question paper 2 Listening	20	30	Approximately 30 minutes
Component 4: assignment – Writing	20	15	No set time limit – centres to use their discretion
Component 5: Performance – Talking	30	30	Approximately 6–8 minutes

DON'T FORGET

Whilst covering the context and topics in each chapter, you will develop your language skills, increase your vocabulary and be given the opportunity to revise grammatical structures. After each topic, you will be asked to use the language learned to write a short essay about the topic. This should help you to consolidate the language learned. You may also wish to use these essays to help prepare your Performance (talking presentation) as part of the external examination.

COMPONENT 1, 2 AND 3: READING AND WRITING; LISTENING

In these components, you will be assessed on all four contexts: society, learning, employability and culture. The question papers for Components 1, 2 and 3 are set and marked by SQA and conducted in your school/college/university under exam conditions in either May or June.

QUESTION PAPER 1 – READING AND WRITING (50 MARKS)

This question paper will assess the skills of reading and writing. The question paper will have two sections:

- reading – 30 marks
- writing – 20 marks, scaled mark 15

Section 1 (reading)

You will read three texts and demonstrate your understanding by providing answers in English to the questions asked.

Each text will be based on one of the four contexts (society, learning, employability, culture) and all the texts will be of equal length and difficulty.

contd

This section is worth a total of 30 marks, with each text being worth 10 marks. There will be 1–2 supported marks in each text.

There will be a variety of question styles and you will be allowed to use a dictionary.

Section 2 (writing)

You will be required to write an email of 120–150 words in Spanish in response to a job advert. There will be four predictable bullet points and two less predictable bullet points. You should have prepared for this thoroughly beforehand and should feel fully equipped to tackle this paper. You will, however, be allowed to use a dictionary.

For help with this section, refer to pages 82–93 of this book.

QUESTION PAPER 2 – LISTENING (20 MARKS, SCALED MARK 30)

You will listen to one monologue in Spanish worth 8 marks and one short conversation in Spanish worth 12 marks. You will demonstrate your understanding by providing short answers in English to the questions asked.

This paper will be based on the context which was not covered in Question paper 1. For example, if the reading texts cover society, culture and learning then the listening paper will be on employability.

This paper is worth a total of 20 marks and there will be a total of 2–3 supported marks, one of which will be in the monologue and will relate to the speaker's 'intent/reason/ attitude/opinion'.

Read about Components 4 and 5 on pp 94–95 of this book.

HOW THIS BOOK CAN HELP YOU

BrightRED Study Guide: National 5 Spanish focuses on your work in the year leading up to the examination. It offers you a study 'toolkit' containing: revision of the National 5 course; progression through contexts and suggested topics; development of language skills; effective techniques for handling exam questions and a range of ways to revise, either on your own or with friends.

Chapter 1: Society	Chapter 2: Learning	Chapter 3: Employability	Chapter 4: Culture	Chapter 5: Writing
Society covers the language needed to discuss relationships with family and friends; healthy lifestyles and illnesses related to an unhealthy lifestyle; media and the impact of reality shows and new technology on our lives; citizenship and the importance of learning foreign languages; the environment and the differences between town and country life and your local area as a tourist centre.	**Learning** covers the language needed to discuss education and exam preparation; different education systems and learners' responsibilities.	**Employability** covers the language needed to discuss different jobs, including part-time work; cover letters, CVs and job applications, and reviewing achievements and evaluating experiences.	**Culture** covers the language needed to discuss your best holiday/trip; the importance of travelling; aspects of other countries, including special events and occasions and literature/films.	**Writing** covers the language you will need to allow you to feel fully prepared for the Writing paper in the exam. This includes personal details (name, age, where you live); school/college education experience until now; skills/interests you have which make you right for the job; related work experience and possible examples of the two unpredictable bullet points.

BEYOND THE EXAM

Not only will this book help you to prepare for and do well in National 5 Spanish, it will also help lay down the skills you will need to do well next year if you decide to continue with Higher Spanish or study a new modern language at Higher or National 5, take Modern Languages for Work Purposes Units, go into further study or training, or to continue into the world of work.

 DON'T FORGET

It is now up to you. We hope this book will prove useful and help prepare you fully for the Course assessments. ¡Buena suerte!

FAMILY AND FRIENDS – LA FAMILIA Y LOS AMIGOS 1

The Society context can cover a wide range of topics. We will look at each topic in turn within this context and develop your 'toolkit' of language skills, knowledge of vocabulary and grammar. The themes will include:

- relationships with family and friends
- conflicts at home
- healthy lifestyles
- lifestyle-related illnesses
- media

- technology
- life in town compared to life in the countryside
- your home area as a tourist centre
- environment.

LET'S GET STARTED!

Let's start with the subject of family and friends. Can you think of what you would like to be able to say about your relationships with your family and friends?

Ideal relationships: ideal parents, ideal brothers and sisters, ideal friendships

What they are like: physical description, personal qualities (positive and negative)

Your relationship with them: why you get on well, what you do together

Who they are: personal information (name, age, description)

Family and friends

Any conflicts there might be: the reasons for arguments

Influences: peer pressure, other people who influence you

Knowledge about language: present tense of regular and irregular verbs, adjective agreements, negatives, conditional tense, tener phrases

YOUR FAMILY AND FRIENDS, WHO ARE THEY? – TU FAMILIA Y TUS AMIGOS, ¿QUIÉNES SON?

Quiz

Can you remember the vocabulary in Spanish for the following?

- Members of the family
- What he or she is called
- What age someone is (don't forget to use *tener* for age!)
- Numbers, days and months
- When someone's birthday is

DON'T FORGET +

This is a perfect opportunity to revise vocabulary that you have previously learned.

THE PRESENT TENSE – EL PRESENTE

When talking about your family relationships, you will mostly use the **present tense**. There are **regular** and **irregular** verbs that you will need to know. Take the following steps to form regular verbs:

1 Write down the **infinitive** without the *-ar, -er* or *-ir* ending (this is known as the stem of the **verb**).

2 Add the present tense ending (this must correspond to the subject).

Example:

amar – to love (this is known as the infinitive)

Chop off the *-ar* to form the stem: *am*

Write the root and add the correct *-ar* verb ending for the subject: I love – *amo*

IRREGULAR VERBS – LOS VERBOS IRREGULARES

Let's move on to irregular verbs. You need to know these off by heart, as they do not follow a pattern. The most important ones that you must learn are:

tener – to have
salir – to go out/to come out
ir – to go
ser – to be
querer – to want/to want to/to love

estar – to be
poder – to be able to/can
hacer – to do/to make
saber – to know/to know how to

Note

Ser is generally used for a permanent condition. Example: *Soy humano; Soy española; Soy serio; Soy alta.*

We normally use *estar* to describe temporary states, emotions or saying where you are. For example: *Estoy comiendo; Estoy triste; Estoy en Madrid.*

THINGS TO DO AND THINK ABOUT

Now that you are a 'present tense expert', try to fill in the gaps with the verbs in the brackets. Remember that you will need to conjugate the verbs, so pay attention to the subject of each sentence:

Yo _____ a mi familia. *(amar)*

Mi familia y yo siempre _____ juntos. *(comer)*

Mis primos _____ en Madrid. *(vivir)*

Mi tío _____ tocar la guitarra. *(saber)*

Yo _____ mucho a mis abuelos. *(querer)*

Mi padrastro _____ cantar y pintar. *(poder)*

Tú _____ una familia numerosa. *(tener)*

Tú y tu familia _____ al cine los fines de semana. *(ir)*

Yo _____ muy feliz porque mi familia ____ muy unida. *(ser, estar)*

Mi hermana _____ los deberes con mi madrastra. *(hacer)*

Tus hermanastros y tú siempre _____ en casa. *(estar)*

ONLINE TEST

Test your memory of all the endings for regular *-ar, -er* and *-ir* verbs at www.brightredbooks.net/N5Spanish

VIDEO LINK

Check out the clip *En mi familia* at www.brightredbooks.net/N5Spanish

FAMILY AND FRIENDS – LA FAMILIA Y LOS AMIGOS 2

WHAT IS HE/SHE LIKE? ¿CÓMO ES ÉL/ELLA?

ONLINE TEST

Head to www.brightredbooks.
net for more examples.

You might want to describe what members of your family or your friends look like. Try to think back to when you learned to describe someone's height, hair and eyes.

> **EXAMPLE:**
> Mi madre es bajit**a**, mi hermana tiene los ojos negr**os** y el pelo larg**o**.

	Masculine	Feminine	Plural masculine	Plural feminine
Adjectives ending in -o	<u>Basic form:</u> generos**o** Él es generoso	Change -*o* into -*a* Ella es generos**a**	Add -*s* Ellos son generos**os**	Change -*o* into -*as* Ellas son generos**as**
Adjectives ending in -a	<u>basic form:</u> optimist**a** Él/Ella es optimista		Add -*s* Ellos/Ellas son optimista**s**	
Adjectives ending in -e	<u>basic form:</u> amabl**e** Él/Ella es amable		Add -*s* Ellos/Ellas son amable**s**	
Most adjectives ending in consonant	<u>basic form:</u> leal, marrón ... Él/Ella es leal Tiene el pelo marrón		Add -*es* Ellos / Ellas son leal**es** Tienen los ojos marron**es** *Notice that the accent disappears	

Notice that the changes are applied to the basic form of the adjective.

Use your dictionary to check the gender of nouns if you are unsure.

Learning vocabulary

Firstly, read through the following adjectives and cover up the English meanings. If you know some words already, put a tick or a green mark beside these words. If there are some words that you think you could guess because they look like English words, put a dash or an orange mark beside these words. Be careful, some of them might be **false friends!**

If there are some words that you don't recognise, put a cross or a red mark beside these words and, when you are doing your revision, spend more time going over and learning these words.

You can listen to these adjectives online to help you with the pronunciation.

DON'T FORGET

When describing someone or something remember that **adjectives** in Spanish must agree! The table above will guide you.

DON'T FORGET

It might be an idea to revise the verb *ser* here, as you will need to know it to describe what someone's personality is like. Let's start with the positives.

Positive adjectives	English meaning
abierto(a)	open
agradable	pleasant
amable	kind
animado(a)	lively
atento(a)	thoughtful
bromista	joker
comprensivo(a)	understanding
divertido(a)	fun
dulce	gentle
educado(a)	polite
generoso(a)	generous
hablador(a)	chatty
inteligente	intelligent
lleno(a) de vida	full of life
paciente	patient
sensato(a)	sensible
sensible	sensitive
simpático(a)	nice

⚙ ACTIVITY: Negatives – La negación

You can use any of these **adjectives** in a negative sentence. All you need to do is put a negative word (*no, nunca, nada, nadie* ...) before the verb.

Here is a reminder of some useful **negatives**. Translate the following sentences and then try to make up five new phrases using positive adjectives in a negative sentence.

no ...　　　　not
Mi hermano mayor no es paciente.
nunca ...　　　never
Mi madre nunca es habladora.
ya no ...　　　not any more
Mi padre ya no es irritante, ahora me escucha.

nadie ...　　　no one
En mi casa nadie es comprensivo.
no ... nada　　not a bit
Mi hermana mayor no es nada generosa.

NEGATIVE ADJECTIVES – ADJETIVOS NEGATIVOS

Once you feel confident using these phrases, move on to the negative adjectives.

Negative adjectives	English meaning	Negative adjectives	English meaning
aburrido(a)	boring	irritante	irritating
anticuado(a)	old-fashioned	malo(a)	mean
antipático(a)	unpleasant	mandón(a)	bossy
arrogante	arrogant	mimado(a)	spoilt
estricto(a)	strict	perezoso(a)	lazy
gruñón(a)	grumpy	pesado(a)	annoying
impaciente	impatient	tonto(a)	silly
infantil	childish	vago(a)	lazy

You might like to add some **qualifiers/intensifiers**:

bastante – quite
un poco – a bit
muy – very

realmente – really
demasiado – too

THINGS TO DO AND THINK ABOUT

Write a paragraph about the members of your family and include names, ages, birthdays and physical descriptions. This could be used as part of your Performance and it is worthwhile revision.

You could start your paragraph by saying how many people there are in your family:
- En mi familia somos _____ personas.

Then you could say their names, ages and birthdays.
- Mi padre se llama ____ y tiene ____ años. Su cumpleaños es el (day) de (month). Mi madrastra se llama ____ y tiene ...

Add their physical description, for example:
- Mi padrastro es bastante alto y tiene los ojos azules y el pelo rizado.

Write a second paragraph describing their personalities. Don't forget to use negatives and qualifiers in your writing.
- Mi hermana es muy (+ adjective) pero a veces puede ser (+ adjective).
- Mi hermanastro no es (+ adjective); sin embargo, es bastante (+ adjective).

LISTENING

Audio tracks to support these activities are available free at www.brightredpublishing.co.uk and www.brightredbooks.net/N5Spanish

DON'T FORGET

A **false friend** is a word in Spanish that looks like a word in English but means something different. For example you might guess that *sensible* in Spanish means 'sensible' in English, but it actually means 'sensitive'.

ONLINE TEST

Take the 'Negative and positive adjectives' test online at www.brightredbooks.net/N5Spanish

VIDEO LINK

Watch the 'Family language and introductions' clip at www.brightredbooks.net/N5Spanish

RELATIONSHIPS – LAS RELACIONES

Think about why you get on well with members of your family or friends and why you sometimes argue with them. It would be useful to learn these important phrases to help you describe your relationships.

POSITIVE RELATIONSHIPS – LAS RELACIONES POSITIVAS

- Tengo una buena relación con ...   I have a good relationship with ...
- Me llevo bien con ...   I get on well with ...
- Me siento cercano(a) a ...   I feel close to ...

It is useful to be able to say why you get on well with family members and friends. Here are some phrases to help:

- ... porque ...
- Mi padre/madre/hermano/hermana es (+ positive adjective).
- (Él/Ella) es (+ positive adjective).

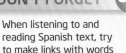

DON'T FORGET

When listening to and reading Spanish text, try to make links with words in English in order to work out the meaning of unfamiliar vocabulary, for example *intereses* looks like 'interests'. By listening to and reading a text, you can also improve your pronunciation.

DON'T FORGET

Remember to check adjective agreements. See page 8, for example: *mi hermano es gracioso/mi hermana es graciosa.*

 **ACTIVITY:** Positive relationships – Las relaciones positivas

Read the following Spanish phrases and match them to the English meanings. You can listen to these phrases online to help you with pronunciation.

1	nos interesamos por las mismas cosas	A	we spend a lot of time together
2	compartimos los mismos intereses	B	he/she is very respectful of my private life
3	tenemos muchas cosas en común	C	he/she respects me
4	(él/ella) tiene un buen sentido del humor	D	we share the same interests
5	pasamos mucho tiempo juntos	E	he/she supports me when I have a problem
6	hacemos todo juntos	F	he/she is always in a good mood
7	salimos juntos a menudo	G	he/she helps me when I need it
8	compartimos buenos momentos	H	we can discuss everything
9	(él/ella) está todos los días de buen humor	I	we do everything together
10	nos reímos juntos	J	we are interested in the same things
11	podemos hablar de todo	K	we have a lot of things in common
12	(él/ella) me respeta	L	we share good times together
13	estamos muy unidos(as)	M	we often go out together
14	(él/ella es) muy respetuoso(a) con mi vida privada	N	we have a laugh together
15	(él/ella) me ayuda cuando lo necesito	O	he/she has a good sense of humour
16	(él/ella) me apoya cuando tengo un problema	P	we are very close

⚙ ACTIVITY: Parental relationships – Las relaciones con los padres

Read the text below first and look up any words you don't know in the dictionary. Then try to predict what you might hear next and think of any Spanish vocabulary that could be used to fill the gaps and complete the sentences.

Then listen to the audio track to hear people talking about the relationships they have with their parents. Fill in the gaps and then translate the phrases into English.

1   Mis padres me dejan _____ con mis _____ todos los fines de semana.

2   Mis padres me dejan bastante_____.

3   Mis padres me_____ mucha ____.

4   Mis padres son muy _____ con mi vida _____.

5   Yo_____ muy bien con mis padres porque ellos _____ en mí.

6   Mis padres son muy _____ y me dan buenos _____.

7   Yo estoy muy _____ a mis padres porque podemos _____ de todo.

8   Tengo suerte porque _____ de todo con mis padres y nos _____ las mismas cosas.

9   Mi madre siempre está de buen _____ y nos _____ juntos.

ONLINE TEST

Take the test 'Relationships – Las relaciones' at www.brightredbooks.net/N5Spanish

VIDEO LINK

Check out the clip 'Getting to know people' at www.brightredbooks.net/N5Spanish

❗ THINGS TO DO AND THINK ABOUT

Adapt any phrases that you like about positive family relationships and write a paragraph to describe your relationships with people in your family. You may wish to learn this paragraph for your Performance.

You could start by saying who you get on well/bad with and why:

Me llevo bien/mal con mi _____ porque ... (+ reasons).

FAMILY CONFLICTS – LOS CONFLICTOS FAMILIARES 1

Although we may get on well with our families, there can be arguments from time to time. What do you tend to argue about with your parents, brothers and sisters? To introduce family conflicts, you may want to start by saying that you don't get on well with someone in particular and then give reasons why. Here are a few ideas.

 ACTIVITY: Negative relationships 1 – Las relaciones negativas 1

Listen to the audio track to hear how these phrases are pronounced then translate them into English.

1 Tengo una mala relación con mi hermana.

2 Tengo una mala relación con mi abuela.

3 Me llevo mal con mi tío.

4 No me entiendo bien con mi hermano.

5 Discuto a menudo con mis padres.

6 De vez en cuando, hay tensión con mis padres.

ACTIVITY: Adverbs – Los adverbios

Can you work out what the underlined words/phrases mean? Use the percentages in brackets as a clue to help you.

1 <u>A menudo</u> (70%) discuto con mi hermano.

2 <u>Siempre</u> (100%) discutimos.

3 <u>A veces</u> (40%) discuto con mi padre.

4 <u>De vez en cuando</u> (30%) discutimos.

5 <u>Raramente</u> (10%) discuto con mi madre.

6 <u>Nunca</u> (0%) discutimos.

Read the phrases again. Can you work out what the rule is for where to place these **adverbs** of frequency?

Note

In Spanish, adverbs of frequency are generally placed at the beginning of the sentence but if the sentence is negative you will need to place the adverb at the end. Example: *Mi hermano y yo no discutimos nunca.*

DON'T FORGET

You can use adverbs of frequency to emphasise how often you argue with your family.

ONLINE TEST ✓

Take the test 'Family conflicts – Los conflictos familiares' at www.brightredbooks.net/N5Spanish

VIDEO LINK ▶

Watch the clip at www.brightredbooks.net/N5 Spanish for more on relationships with parents.

ACTIVITY: Negative relationships 2 – Las relaciones negativas 2

Here are some reasons why there may be conflicts or tensions with your family or friends.

Can you work out what they mean?

Discuto con mis padres/padre/madre/hermano/hermana porque ...

1 mi padre/mi madre/mi hermano/mi hermana es (+ negative adjective).

2 mis padres son (+ adjective – don't forget agreement).

3 (él/ella) es (+ negative adjective).

4 (ellos) son (+ negative adjective – don't forget agreement).

5 (él/ella) coge mi ropa sin pedirme permiso.

6 (él/ella) miente todo el tiempo.

7 mis padres quieren ver programas diferentes en la tele.

contd

8 (él/ella) pone la música muy alta cuando hago los deberes.

9 (él/ella) actúa de forma distinta delante de mis padres.

10 mi padre se burla de mí delante de mis amigos.

11 mis hermanos me irritan todo el tiempo.

12 mi hermana usa mi maquillaje/mi ordenador sin pedirme permiso.

ARGUMENTS – LAS DISCUSIONES

You might want to be more specific about arguments that you may have had with your parents. You can start by talking about general reasons for arguments and then go into more detail. When talking about arguments with your parents, make sure you use the third person plural endings (*ellos*).

THINGS TO DO AND THINK ABOUT

Read the following sentences and work out what they mean. Try to find links between English and Spanish vocabulary to help you work out what the words mean before checking in the dictionary.

Listen to phrases online to help you with pronunciation.

Yo discuto con mis padres por culpa/a causa …
… de los estudios
  - Ellos piensan que no estudio bastante.
  - No están contentos con mis notas en el instituto.
… de las salidas
  - No me dejan salir con mis amigos durante la semana.
  - No me dan suficiente libertad.
… de mis amigos
… de mi novio/novia
  - A ellos no les gusta/n mi novio(a)/mis amigos.
  - Piensan que paso demasiado tiempo con mis amigos.
  - Creen que soy muy joven para tener novio/novia.
… del dinero
  - Ellos no me dan suficiente dinero.
  - Piensan que malgasto mi dinero.
  - No me dejan tener un trabajo a tiempo parcial para ganar dinero.
… de las tareas domésticas
  - Ellos piensan que no hago nada en la casa y que soy demasiado perezoso(a).
  - Creo que ayudo mucho en casa pero ellos no están de acuerdo.
  - Tengo que ayudar mucho en casa pero mi hermana no hace nada.
… de mi vida privada
  - Se meten en mis asuntos.
  - No respetan mi vida privada.
  - Siempre quieren saber lo que pasa en mi vida, eso me pone nervioso(a).
  - Hacen muchas preguntas sobre mis amigos/novio/novia/estudios.
… de mi comportamiento
  - Piensan que soy desobediente.
  - No están contentos con mi comportamiento en casa/el colegio.
… de mis aficiones
  - Piensan que paso demasiado tiempo viendo la televisión/escuchando música/jugando con el ordenador.
  - Dicen que paso demasiado tiempo en internet/con mi móvil/en Facebook.

DON'T FORGET

Can you spot how the verbs change when the subject/person changes from singular to plural? Look back at the present tense summary on page 7 to revise how the endings change.

DON'T FORGET

The infinitive is the name of the verb tense which ends in *-ar*, *-er* or *-ir* in Spanish. The equivalent in English is the 'to' form, for example *mirar* – to look.

ONLINE TEST

Head to www.brightredbooks.net/N5Spanish to test yourself on this topic.

FAMILY CONFLICTS – LOS CONFLICTOS FAMILIARES 2

 **ACTIVITY:** Arguments with parents 1 –
Las discusiones con los padres 1

Read the following texts about why some young people argue with their parents. Try to identify some of the vocabulary we have already covered.

For each text take notes on the following:

1   Who do they not get on with/argue with?

Daniel

Diría que, desafortunadamente, tengo una mala relación con mi padre. Siempre está encima de mí. A menudo discuto con él. Nunca está contento, porque piensa que paso demasiado tiempo con el móvil. No entiende que es que quiero hablar con mi novia, pero el problema es que a él no le gusta mi novia. Cree que soy demasiado joven para tener novia y que debo pasar la mayor parte del tiempo estudiando. Lo que más me molesta es que se mete en mis asuntos y, en mi opinión, tiene que respetar mi vida privada.

2   Why?

Paula

Es cierto que a veces hay conflictos en mi casa a causa de las tareas domésticas y del dinero. Mi madre me critica todo el tiempo y me regaña si no lavo los platos o si no paso la aspiradora. Después de pasar muchas horas en el instituto no tengo ganas de hacer las tareas del hogar. No es justo, porque mi hermano no hace nada en casa. Además, a todos mis amigos sus padres les dan veinte euros a la semana por ayudar en casa. Mi madre no me daría nada si yo no hiciera las tareas domésticas, y eso me molesta. Yo recibo diez euros cada semana y eso no es suficiente.

Put your answers into the table:

	Daniel	Paula
Who does he/she argue with?		
Why?		

 **ACTIVITY:** Arguments with parents 2 –
Las discusiones con los padres 2

Now try to put together some sentences about the arguments you have with your parents.

Here are some starters:

- A menudo discuto con mis padres sobre ...   I often argue with my parents about ...
- Hay tensiones con mis padres por culpa de ...   There are tensions with my parents because of ...
- Con respecto a los conflictos en mi casa, hay discusiones a causa de ...   With regards to conflicts at home, there are arguments about ...
- Lo que me molesta es que en mi casa hay conflictos por culpa de ...   What annoys me is that there are conflicts at home because of ...
- Lo que odio, son las tensiones en mi casa a causa de ...   What I hate are the tensions at home because of ...
- Diría que en mi casa a menudo hay discusiones a causa de ...   I would say that there are often arguments at home because of ...

 THINGS TO DO AND THINK ABOUT

Write a paragraph about any arguments or tensions in your family. You may wish to use this as part of your Performance. Start by saying if there are arguments or tensions in your family and reasons why:

e.g. A veces mis padres y yo discutimos porque yo no quiero ayudar con las tareas domésticas y porque no me gusta estudiar.

 DON'T FORGET

You can adapt and use these phrases in your Performance about your family relationships.

 ONLINE TEST

Take the test 'Family conflicts – Los conflictos familiares' at www.brightredbooksnet/N5Spanish

 VIDEO LINK

For more, watch the clip 'Conflictos de la Familia' at www.brightredbooks.net/N5Spanish

IDEAL PARENTS – LOS PADRES IDEALES

We have talked about reasons why you don't get along with your parents. We will now look at how you would describe your ideal parents. You can recycle some of the language we have already learned in this unit. You will also need to know the **conditional tense.**

- What would be your idea of a perfect parent? What would they be like?

- What would they do and what would they not do?

CONDITIONAL TENSE – EL CONDICIONAL

You will need to know the conditional tense in order to describe your ideal parents. The conditional tense describes what someone would be like or what they would do. It is really easy to form as the endings remain the same for -ar, -er and -ir verbs, although there are some irregular conditional stems that you will need to learn.

1. Write down the infinitive of the verb: *comer*

2. Now add the conditional endings to the infinitive: *Yo comer*ía – I would eat.

The conditional endings are:

Yo:	-ía	Nosotros/Nosotras:	-íamos
Tú:	-ías	Vosotros/Vosotras:	-íais
Él/Ella/Usted:	-ía	Ellos/Ellas/Ustedes:	-ían

The key irregular verbs that you need to know include:

tener – yo tendría (I would have)   poder – yo podría (I would be able to/could)

querer – yo querría (I would want/love)   venir – yo vendría (I would come)

hacer – yo haría (I would do)   saber – yo sabría (I would know)

decir – yo diría (I would say)   salir – yo saldría (I would go out)

 **ACTIVITY:** conditional tense – El condicional

Try to complete the following sentences using the conditional tense of the verb in brackets:

1. Yo _____ la televisión con mi padre. (*ver*)
2. Tú _____ mi tarea. (*terminar*)
3. Ella _____ un libro. (*leer*)
4. Nosotros _____ más tiempo juntos. (*pasar*)
5. Vosotros _____ más a menudo. (*hablar*)

ACTIVITY: Irregular conditional stems – Los verbos irregulares en condicional

Translate the following sentences into Spanish using irregular conditional verbs:

1. Mis padres _____ más tiempo libre. (*tener*)
2. Mi hermano _____ más deporte con mi padre. (*hacer*)
3. Yo _____ con mis amigos durante la semana. (*salir*)
4. Ella _____ más. (*estudiar*)
5. Yo _____ que mi hermana es muy simpática. (*decir*)

IDEAL PARENTS – LOS PADRES IDEALES

Let's start by describing the qualities of an ideal parent: we could use some negatives here as well. Have a look back at the section on negatives (page 9) if you need to revise them again.

ACTIVITY: Ideal parents – Los padres ideales

Listen to the audio track and read the following phrases. Put the phrases in the correct order and translate them into English.

1 Los padres ideales darían bastante libertad a sus hijos.
2 Los padres ideales no se enfadarían fácilmente.
3 Los padres ideales protegerían a sus hijos.
4 Los padres ideales no serían demasiado protectores.
5 Los padres ideales serían pacientes y tolerantes.
6 Los padres ideales no serían anticuados.
7 Los padres ideales siempre estarían disponibles para sus hijos.
8 Los padres ideales pasarían mucho tiempo con sus hijos.
9 Los padres ideales darían buenos consejos a sus hijos.
10 Los padres ideales nunca consentirían a sus hijos.
11 Los padres ideales tendrían confianza en sus hijos.

ONLINE TEST

Take the test 'Ideal parents – Los padres ideales' at www.brightredbooks.net/N5Spanish

ACTIVITY: Ideal parents – Los padres ideales

Now, it's your turn. Choose five phrases that describe positive relationships and five phrases that describe negative relationships with parents and change them into the conditional tense to describe an ideal parent. A couple of examples have been done for you:

1 (Él/Ella) tiene un buen sentido del humor – Los padres ideales tendrían un buen sentido del humor.
2 (Él/Ella) se burla de mí delante de mis amigos – Los padres ideales no se burlarían de sus hijos.

ONLINE

Learn more phrases for talking about your parents at www.brightredbooks.net/N5Spanish

THINGS TO DO AND THINK ABOUT

Write a paragraph about an ideal parent/ideal parents. You may wish to learn this as part of your Performance. You could write about:
- Personalities you would like your ideal parents to have.
- Things you would like your ideal parents to do with you.
- Places you would like your ideal parents to take you to.

Example : Mis padres ideales serían muy divertidos y bastante comprensivos.
Mis padres ideales siempre harían los deberes conmigo.
Mis padres ideales me llevarían al cine a menudo.

FRIENDSHIP – LA AMISTAD

Although we have touched on friendship already and some of the phrases we have learned can be used to describe your friendships, we are now going to focus on how you spend time with your friends, along with peer pressure.

ACTIVITY: Spending time with your family/friends – Pasar tiempo con tu familia/amigos

Listen to the following conversation between two people discussing their friends. Fill in the gaps using the words in the box below. Before listening to the audio track, read through the text and predict what you might hear.

A   Tengo suerte porque mi_____amiga y yo tenemos los mismos_____. Nos lo pasamos bien cuando vamos de _____el sábado por la tarde y por la noche, nos_____ cuando vamos al cine. Nos encanta ver películas_____. Y tú Claudio, ¿pasas mucho tiempo con tus amigos?

B   Ah, sí. Pasamos horas juntos jugando al fútbol porque formamos _____ del mismo club de fútbol. Lo que más me _____es jugar partidos de fútbol el _____ por la mañana con mis amigos.

A   ¿Tienes un mejor amigo?

B   Sí, se llama Felipe y es_____ y realmente simpático. Nos _____ en los mismos deportes, por eso vemos los deportes en la_____. Puedo contar con él y si tengo un problema, me _____ y me da buenos _____ .

A   A mi parecer, lo más importante es que estamos en la misma _____. Me gusta hablar de todo con mi mejor amiga y puedo _____ en ella.

divertido	compras	ayuda	reímos	mejor	gusta	interesamos
consejos	sábado	confiar	cómicas	intereses	tele	parte	onda

DON'T FORGET

You can use any of these phrases to talk about your family relationships by changing the person to a member of your family.

DON'T FORGET

To show off your knowledge of the conditional tense, you could add what a good friend would and would not be like. Refer back to the section on the conditional tense (page 16).

ACTIVITY: Relationships with friends – Las relaciones con los amigos.

Read the following phrases and decide if the phrases are describing a good friend or a bad friend. Listen to the audio track to help with pronunciation. You might want to practise translating the phrases into English.

(Él/Ella) me entiende.

(Él/Ella) no me critica.

(Él/Ella) raramente me anima.

(Él/Ella) no me apoya nunca.

(Él/Ella) me irrita/molesta.

(Él/Ella) no es pesado(a).

(Él/Ella) nunca es celoso(a).

(Él/Ella) me aburre.

(Él/Ella) tiene sentido del humor.

(Él/Ella) se queja todo el tiempo.

(Él/Ella) no es egoísta.

(Él/Ella) me respeta.

(Él/Ella) no me escucha nunca.

(Yo) puedo confiar en ella.

(Él/Ella) me ignora en el colegio.

(Él/Ella) siempre está ahí cuando necesito a alguien.

(Él/Ella) discute por todo.

⚙ ACTIVITY: Translating the conditional tense

Put the phrases above into the conditional tense to describe what a good friend would do, then translate them into English. You might need to turn some phrases into negative sentences (refer back to the notes on negatives on page 9).

Here are a few to start you off:

1 Un buen amigo me entendería.
2 Un buen amigo **no me criticaría**.
3 Él/Ella me apoyaría.

Write a paragraph about your friends. You might want to include what makes a good friend and how you spend time with your friends. You may wish to use this as part of your Performance.

⚙ ACTIVITY: Peer pressure – La presión del grupo

When we are talking about friendships, peer pressure often arises as a topic for discussion. Read the following phrases and decide if the person in each sentence is influenced by his/her peers or not.

- Me gusta sentirme a gusto con mis amigos, por eso hago lo que hacen ellos.
- Hago lo que quiero sin preocuparme de lo que piensen otros jóvenes.
- Me siento mejor cuando estoy en un grupo de amigos.
- Tengo miedo de las opiniones y juicios de los demás.
- Tengo ganas de ser original y diferente de mis amigos.
- No quiero sentirme aislado(a) o solo(a).
- Tengo la costumbre de vestirme como mis amigos.
- Tengo suerte porque no presto atención a lo que piensan mis amigos.
- Lo que más me gusta es que llevamos la ropa que queremos.
- Llevo mal mostrar mi personalidad a mis amigos.
- Tengo ganas de formar parte de un grupo musical para ser como los otros.
- Tengo la necesidad de comprar la ropa de marca.
- Tengo la oportunidad de salir con mis amigos todos los fines de semana y no me gustaría quedar excluido(a).
- Tengo suerte porque mis amigos no me juzgan nunca.
- Fumo como todos mis amigos para ser más guay/cool.
- Siempre sigo a mis amigos, quienes me irritan de vez en cuando.
- Tengo suerte porque puedo identificarme con mis amigos pero no necesitamos tener los mismos gustos.
- Me cuesta resistirme a la presión del grupo porque no quiero ser diferente.

❗ THINGS TO DO AND THINK ABOUT

From the sentences about peer pressure, can you pick out any *tener* **phrases**? Here are some useful *tener* phrases. Do you know what they mean?

Tener necesidad de	Tener la oportunidad de	Tener hambre
Tener ganas de	Tener suerte porque	Tener calor
Tener miedo de	Tener sed	Tener frío

Make up nine sentences, one for each of these *tener* phrases.

For example: Cuando termino las clases, siempre tengo hambre.

ONLINE TEST

Take the test 'Friendship – La amistad' at www.brightredbooks.net/N5Spanish

VIDEO LINK

Check out the clip 'Meeting new friends' at www.brightredbooks.net/N5Spanish

DON'T FORGET

A peer is a person of the same age or status as you. Your classmates at school can be described as your peers.

DON'T FORGET

Lo/los que and *quien/quienes* are called '**relative pronouns**'. You will notice *lo que* y *quienes* in these phrases. Can you work out what they mean?

PEOPLE WHO INFLUENCE ME – LAS PERSONAS QUE ME INFLUYEN

PHRASES THAT EXPRESS WHO INFLUENCES YOU AND WHY

If you are asked who influences you, you might think of a member of your family. Here are some phrases to express who influences you and why.

- Mi familia me inspira. – My family inspires me.
- Mi familia me influye, cada uno a su manera. – My family influences me, each in their own way.
- Mi hermano juega un papel muy importante en mi vida. – My brother plays a very important role in my life.
- Pienso que mi madre me influye mucho. – I think that my mum influences me a lot.
- La persona que más me influye es mi padre. – The person who influences me the most is my dad.
- Mis padres pueden influir en mis elecciones. – My parents can influence my choices.
- Una persona que me influye en la vida es mi abuelo. – A person who influences me in my life is my grandfather.
- Mi mejor amigo(a) influye en mis decisiones. – My best friend influences my decisions.

Here are some reasons why:

- … porque (él/ella) es una persona sensata. – because he/she is wise.
- … porque paso la mayor parte de mi tiempo libre con él/ella. – Because I spend most of my free time with him/her.
- …porque lo/la respeto. – because I respect him/her.
- …porque (él/ella) me da buenos consejos. – because he/she gives me good advice.
- …porque (él/ella) siempre tiene razón. – because he/she is always right.

DON'T FORGET

Remember to adapt the phrases and learn them so you can choose to use them in your Performance.

ONLINE TEST

Take the test 'People who influence me – Las personas que me influyen' at www.brightredbooks.net/N5Spanish

⚙ **ACTIVITY:** Peer pressure and influence

Write a paragraph about whether or not you feel peer pressure and about the people who influence you. Again, this could be used as part of your Performance.

RELATIONSHIPS WITH FAMILY AND FRIENDS: RECAP

By the end of this section, you should have written various paragraphs on the following topics:

Who is in your family: personal information (name, age, description)

What are they like: physical description, personal qualities (positive and negative)

Your relationships with them: why you get on well, what you do together

Any conflicts there might be: the reasons for arguments

Ideal relationships: ideal parents, ideal brothers and sisters, ideal friendships

Influences: peer pressure, other people who influence you

You should also feel confident about the following grammar points:

- present tense of regular and irregular verbs
- adjective agreements
- negatives
- conditional tense
- *tener* phrases.

Test yourself: Vocabulary

Can you recall and write down:

- three positive adjectives?
- three negative adjectives?
- three positive phrases about your relationship with your family?
- three negative phrases about your relationship with your family?
- three phrases about ideal parents?
- three phrases about what you do with your friends/family?
- three phrases about peer pressure?

Test yourself: Knowledge about language

Can you recall:

- the rule about adjective agreements?
- six negatives?
- how to form the conditional tense?
- three *tener* phrases?
- three adverbs of frequency?
- what *quien/quienes* and *lo/los que* mean?

VIDEO LINK

Learn more by watching the clip 'Talking about your family' at www.brightredbooks.net/N5Spanish

THINGS TO DO AND THINK ABOUT

You have learned a lot in this section and used your listening, reading, dictionary and writing skills, as well as learning vocabulary and grammar rules. Following the 'Test yourself' tasks, is there any area that you are not sure of? If so, look over this section again and revise the vocabulary or grammar that is causing you difficulty.

LEISURE – EL TIEMPO LIBRE 1

You will know quite a lot of vocabulary already about *tiempo libre,* like different types of sports and hobbies. When thinking about your hobbies, you could mention the following:

¿Cuándo? ¿Opinión? ¿Dónde? **Mi pasatiempo favorito es ...** ¿Con quién? ¿Por qué?

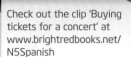 **ACTIVITY:** Revision – Repaso

It is useful to be able to say how often you do your hobbies, when, with whom, why and where. You could include this in a piece of writing or as part of your Performance.

Here are a few phrases to start you off. Can you work out what they mean?

Mi pasatiempo favorito es ...

jugar al tenis	ir al cine	practicar la equitación
practicar la natación	ir de compras/tiendas	leer
ver la tele	escuchar música	hacer deporte/ejercicio

¿Con quién?

con mis amigos(as)	formo parte de un equipo
con mi madre/padre	yo solo(a)
soy miembro de un club	

DON'T FORGET

It can be useful to revise the verbs *hacer, jugar* and *practicar* as they are very commonly used when we talk about free time in Spanish.

¿Cúando?

el sábado por la mañana
una vez por/a la semana
de vez en cuando
el martes después de clase
tres veces por/al mes
raramente
el miércoles por la noche
a menudo
el domingo por la tarde
a veces

¿Dónde?

en el parque
en el centro de la ciudad
en el polideportivo
en el campo de fútbol/golf
en mi casa
en el jardín

¿Opinión?

me encanta
me gusta
me apasiona
me interesa

¿Por qué?

es divertido(a)
me ayuda a relajarme
es apasionante
es una buena manera de librarme del estrés de la vida escolar
es entretenido(a)
es bueno(a) para la salud
es relajante
me mantiene en forma
puedo conocer a gente nueva

 DON'T FORGET

Look at the section on healthy living to find more reasons for why you do your hobbies.

HOBBIES – LOS PASATIEMPOS

The following list is a reminder of some of the more difficult vocabulary to do with hobbies. Can you remember what the following words/phrases mean? If not, look up any unfamiliar vocabulary in the dictionary.

montar a caballo	nadar
ir de compras	leer novelas
practicar ciclismo	salir con mis amigos
practicar ciclismo de montaña	pasar tiempo con mis amigos
practicar escalada	ir a una fiesta/a la discoteca/de marcha
practicar vela	ir al cine/teatro/a la piscina
practicar buceo	ver la tele/películas
practicar senderismo	escuchar música en mi iPod
practicar deportes acuáticos	pasar tiempo en internet/en Facebook
ir de tiendas	hablar con mis amigos por el móvil
ir de paseo	hacer visita a alguien
montar en bicicleta/barco	jugar al baloncesto

 THINGS TO DO AND THINK ABOUT

Don't forget to revise the irregular verbs.

To describe what you do during your free time, you need to know verbs in the present tense. Refer to page 7 to revise how to form the present tense with *-ar*, *-er* and *-ir* verbs.

 ONLINE TEST

Why not try the 'Irregular verbs' online test to revise these, including *ir* y *hacer* at www.brightredbooks.net/N5Spanish

LEISURE – EL TIEMPO LIBRE 2

TO DO SPORT – HACER DEPORTE

To say which sports you do, you need to know the verbs *jugar* and *practicar*.

If the sport:	jugar		practicar
Is masculine	Verb is followed by *al* (contraction of <u>a + el</u>), for example: • Juego al fútbol		Verb is followed by the name of the sport, for example: • Practico natación • Él practica boxeo
Is feminine	Verb is followed by *a la*, for example: • Juego a la pelota vasca		

Note

Jugar is normally used when we talk about sports considered as games, such as *fútbol*, *baloncesto*, *golf*, etc. For other sports such as *natación*, *ciclismo*, *boxeo*, etc, *practicar* is normally used.

VIDEO LINK

Have a look at the clip 'Hobbies' at www.brightredbooks.net/N5Spanish

ACTIVITY: To do sport – Hacer deporte

Translate the following sentences into Spanish. In some of them you should use *practicar* and in others *jugar* and *al* or *a la*.

1 I play football.
2 He goes swimming.
3 She goes horse riding.
4 We play handball.
5 They (masculine) go sailing.
6 I go hiking.
7 You (formal) play golf.
8 They (feminine) go cycling.

TO GO TO THE TOWN CENTRE – IR AL CENTRO DE LA CIUDAD

Ir is another very important irregular verb that you need to know. There are different ways of saying 'to the' in Spanish depending on whether the place is:

- masculine, for example *el parque* – *voy al parque* (remember *a + el = al*)
- feminine, for example *la piscina* – *voy a la piscina*
- plural and masculine, for example *los comercios* – *voy a los comercios*
- plural and feminine, for example *las tiendas* – *voy a las tiendas*.

ACTIVITY: To go to the ... – Ir al/a la/a los/a las ...

Translate the following sentences into Spanish using the correct part of *ir* and *al, a la, a los* or *a las*.

1 I am going to the cinema.

2 He is going to the sports centre.

3 She is going to the beach.

4 We are going to the shops.

5 They (masculine) are going to the theatre.

6 I am going to the shopping centre.

7 You (formal) are going to the restaurant.

8 They (feminine) are going to the hotel.

ACTIVITY: Opinions – Las opiniones

It is a good idea to revise how to give your opinion in more detail at this stage. Read and listen to the following passage and pick out all the **opinion phrases**. You may wish to include them in your writing and Performance.

Joaquín

Creo que soy muy deportista. Me encanta pasar mi tiempo libre haciendo deporte. Mi deporte preferido es el baloncesto. Lo que más me gusta es jugar al baloncesto con mis amigos porque nos divierte jugar en equipo. Pienso que a mi hermana no le gusta el baloncesto. Prefiere nadar, porque dice que es bueno para la salud. Se entrena tres veces a la semana y le encanta. Yo, en cambio, odio la natación porque me canso y lo encuentro muy molesto. A mi padre también le interesa el deporte y pasamos horas viendo deporte en la tele. Cree que eso ayuda a relajarse después de la jornada laboral. Mi madre odia ver el deporte en la televisión. Prefiere ver películas románticas y a mí me parece aburrido. De hecho, prefiere pasar horas leyendo una buena novela en lugar de ver la tele. Piensa que es una buena manera de escapar de la rutina.

As well as picking out the key opinion phrases, can you note down what each person enjoys doing in their free time and why?

 ONLINE TEST

Try the 'Tiempo libre – Los pasatiempos' test online at www.brightredbooks.net/N5Spanish

DON'T FORGET

If you are unsure whether a verb is regular or irregular, check the verb section in your bilingual dictionary. This section will also give you examples of the verb formed in different tenses.

THINGS TO DO AND THINK ABOUT

You should revise other sports and hobbies, opinions and adverbs of time in Spanish at this stage to refresh your memory. Write a paragraph on how you spend your free time and try to include more elaborate phrases. Here are some examples:

- When you do the hobbies. *(por la noche, por la mañana, en verano, en invierno ...)*
- How often you do the hobbies. *(tres veces por a la semana, cada viernes, a menudo ...)*
- Where you do the hobbies. *(en el parque, en el polideportivo, en casa ...)*
- With whom you do the hobbies. *(con mi hermano, con mis amigos, yo solo/a ...)*
- Why you do the hobbies. *(es interesante, divertido, emocionante, entretenido ...)*

You might also want to refer to the section on using technology and the internet in your free time (refer to pages 38-9). This paragraph can be used as a piece of writing and also as part of your Performance.

HEALTHY LIFESTYLE – ESTILO DE VIDA SALUDABLE 1

In this section you will learn to talk about what you do to stay healthy. We will divide it into what physical exercise we do and what we eat and drink to keep healthy.

USEFUL VOCABULARY

Here is some useful vocabulary that will help you to describe how to stay healthy. Spend a few minutes looking at this vocabulary and then cover up the English meanings. How many of these words can you remember? Revise the ones that you are having difficulty with and then cover the English again to see if you can remember them all. Leave it for a while and then come back to this vocabulary. How many can you remember now?

Hay que + infinitive	It is necessary to/you must
No hay que + infinitive	It is not necessary to/you must not
Se debe + infinitive	We must
No se debe + infinitive	We must not
Beber agua	Drink water
Controlar el estrés	Control stress
Dormir	Sleep
Estar sano	To be in good health
Hacer ejercicio	Do exercise
Cuidar la salud	Take care of your health
Hacer deporte	Do sport
Comer cinco porciones de fruta o verdura al día	Eat five portions of fruit and vegetables per day
Comer alimentos frescos	Eat fresh food
Tener una vida activa	Lead an active life
Mantenerse en forma	Stay fit
Seguir una dieta sana/saludable	Follow a healthy diet
Seguir una dieta equilibrada	Follow a balanced diet
Encontrar equilibrio entre el trabajo y el tiempo libre	Find the balance between work and leisure
Evitar los dulces	Avoid sweet things
Evitar las comidas grasas	Avoid fatty foods
Ganar peso/Engordar	Put on weight

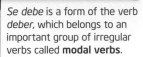

DON'T FORGET

Hay que can be used in lots of different contexts. It is followed by the infinitive.

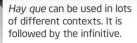

DON'T FORGET

Se debe is a form of the verb *deber*, which belongs to an important group of irregular verbs called **modal verbs**.

MODAL VERBS

A modal verb is a verb associated with possibility or necessity, such as 'can, could, may, might, must, shall, should, will' and 'would'. In Spanish the most common modal verbs are:

querer – to want to
Quiero jugar al fútbol. – I want to play football.

deber – must/should
Debo comer de forma sana. – I must eat healthily.
Deberíamos comer de forma sana. – We should eat healthily.

poder – to be able to/can
Yo puedo hacer deporte. – I am able/can do sport.
Podríamos comer más verduras. – We could eat more vegetables.

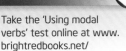

ONLINE TEST

Take the 'Using modal verbs' test online at www.brightredbooks.net/N5Spanish

contd

saber – to know how to
Sé comer de forma sana. – I know how to eat healthily.
Sabemos llevar una vida activa. – We know how to lead an active life.

soler – I usually/normally ...
Suelo beber tres litros de agua al día – I usually drink three litres of water a day.
Note: Soler is also commonly used in the past tense:
Antes, solía nadar diariamente – Before, I used to swim daily.

VIDEO LINK

Revise this further by watching the clip at www.brightredbooks.net/N5Spanish

 **ACTIVITY:** Opinions – Las opiniones

Read the following text and answer the questions in English. Here are some tips for how to approach a reading text for the Course and Unit reading assessments:

- It's useful to read the questions first. This will give you an idea of what the text is about before you even begin to read the Spanish.
- You might want to think about the type of vocabulary you are looking for in the text, for example if the question asks you when something happens you will need to think about time phrases.
- Looking at the number of marks given for each answer will indicate how much information you need to look for.
- When you skim the text, find the parts of the passage that answer the questions by spotting key words.
- Then take each question at a time and read the text more closely, looking up any unfamiliar vocabulary in the dictionary.

Pedro

Para tener una buena salud, es importante tener una dieta equilibrada. Hay que variar la alimentación y evitar los alimentos grasos y azucarados como las pizzas, las patatas fritas y el chocolate, porque si comemos alimentos con demasiada grasa y con demasiado azúcar, podemos volvernos obesos. La obesidad puede llevar a enfermedades como la diabetes, o enfermedades del corazón. Debemos comer carne o pescado, porque tienen proteínas y hierro. Además, debemos tomar frutas y verduras, ya que contienen fibra, vitaminas y minerales. No debemos olvidar tomar productos lácteos, como la leche y el queso, porque aportan calcio, que es importante para el cuerpo. Y también hay que beber al menos dos litros de agua al día y evitar tomar demasiada cafeína o alcohol, con el fin de mantenerse sano. Pienso que se puede comer de todo, pero en cantidades razonables.

1 Why does Pedro think eating a balanced diet is important? (1)
2 What does he think you should avoid and why? (2)
3 What can obesity lead to? (2)
4 What do meat and fish provide us with? (2)
5 What should we eat in order to have fibre, vitamins and minerals? (2)
6 Which two examples of dairy products does Pedro mention? (2)
7 What does Pedro say about water? (2)
8 What does he think you should avoid drinking? (2)

ONLINE

Head to www.brightredbooks.net for a further reading activity.

THINGS TO DO AND THINK ABOUT

Take a note of any useful phrases about what to eat and drink to stay healthy, and what to avoid. If you learn them, you will be able to use them in your Performance.

HEALTHY LIFESTYLE – ESTILO DE VIDA SALUDABLE 2

Now we will look at other ways of staying healthy and focus on doing physical exercise and keeping fit.

 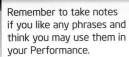

⚙ ACTIVITY: Keeping fit – Mantenerse en forma

Listen to three people talking about what they do to keep fit. Fill in the blanks using the vocabulary in the boxes below each section. Read through the text first and try to predict what you might hear. Use a dictionary to look up any unfamiliar vocabulary.

Alejandro

Para estar en forma, hay que hacer _____ regularmente y seguir una _____ sana. A mí me gusta el tenis y he jugado _____ cinco años. Soy muy _____ y me divierto cuando juego al tenis con mis amigos. Cuando era más joven, jugaba al golf con mi padre. En verano, pasaba horas en el _____ . Creo que ahora tengo demasiados deberes que hacer, así que no tengo suficiente tiempo para _____ al golf y al tenis. Tengo que elegir entre los dos deportes y como ninguno de mis amigos juega al golf, he decidido _____ jugando al tenis. Yo no paso mucho tiempo delante de _____ , como la tele o el ordenador, porque me doy cuenta de que si queremos _____ en forma, debemos hacer ejercicio físico.

ejercicio físico	jugar	continuar	dieta	durante
pantallas	mantenernos	competitivo	campo de golf	

Begoña

Debo admitir que no soy muy _____ . No me gusta nada el deporte y prefiero leer un buen libro o ver una película en el cine ya que eso __ _____ . No tengo la motivación para ir al _____ o para hacer deporte. En el instituto, juego al _____ durante las clases de educación física. Es divertido pero muy agotador. Para mantenerme en forma, voy al instituto _____ en lugar de coger el autobús. Además subo las _____ andando en lugar de usar el _____ . Yo sé que una falta de actividad física puede ser el origen de _____ . Cuando sea más mayor, no quiero volverme _____ . Por eso, cuando termine el instituto, tengo la _____ de hacer más ejercicio físico

gimnasio	activa	me relaja	obesa	ascensor
baloncesto	enfermedades	andando	intención	escaleras

Antonio

Lo que más me gusta es la _____ . Soy miembro de un club y voy a _____ cuatro veces por semana. La semana pasada participé en un _____ de natación. No gané pero _____ divertido porque tengo amigos que forman parte del mismo club de natación. El próximo viernes tendré otra competición. El entrenamiento comienza a las seis de la mañana, por eso, antes de ir al instituto debo _____ temprano e ir a la _____ . Es importante _____ bastante temprano también, siempre antes de las diez. Creo que la natación me ayuda a controlar el estrés y, en mi opinión, hay que encontrar el _____ entre el trabajo en el instituto y el tiempo libre. Tengo suerte porque no me pongo _____ a menudo, gracias a mi vida activa y sana

enfermo	campeonato	natación	piscina	levantarme
entrenar	fue	acostarse	equilibrio	

KNOWLEDGE ABOUT LANGUAGE

In the listening texts, you heard phrases in the **preterite** (*jugué*), **simple future** (*tendré*) and the **imperfect tense** (*era*).

The simple future – El futuro simple

The simple future tense is used to describe an action that will happen in the future. It is similar to the conditional tense in how it is formed:

1   Write down the infinitive: *jugar*
2   Now add the simple future endings to the infinitive: *jugar*é – I will play

The simple future endings are:

Yo:	-é	Nosotros/Nosotras:	-emos
Tú:	-ás	Vosotros/Vosotras:	-éis
Él/Ella/Usted:	-á	Ellos/Ellas/Ustedes:	-án

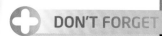

DON'T FORGET

To revise the imperfect tense see page 47. To revise the preterite see page 69.

 ACTIVITY: The simple future – El futuro simple

Now translate the following sentences using the simple future tense:
1   I will spend less time watching TV.
2   I will eat healthily.
3   I will play football with my friends.
4   We will drink two litres of water per day.
5   We will avoid fatty foods.

IRREGULAR FUTURE STEMS

They have the same endings as the regular *-er* and *-ir* verbs but the stem is different:

tener	➡ tendr	decir	➡ dir
venir	➡ vendr	querer	➡ querr
poder	➡ podr	hacer	➡ har
saber	➡ sabr	salir	➡ saldr

Here you have a couple of them conjugated to help you out:

tener	**decir**
tend**ré** (I will have)	di**ré** (I will say)
tend**rás** (you will have)	di**rás** (you will say)
tend**rá** (he, she, it will have)	di**rá** (he, she, it will say)
tend**remos** (we will have)	di**remos** (we will say)
tend**réis** (you will have)	di**réis** (you will say)
tend**rán** (they will have)	di**rán** (they will say)

 ACTIVITY: Irregular verbs in the simple future tense –
Los verbos irregulares en el futuro simple

Translate the following sentences into Spanish using the irregular future stems:
1   I will want to eat less fatty foods.
2   I will do more sport.
3   I will have to do more physical exercise.
4   We will be able to stay fit.
5   We will be more active.

ONLINE

To find out more about irregular verbs conjugated in the simple future tense, go to the Bright Red Digital Zone online at www.brightredbooks.net/ N5Spanish

THINGS TO DO AND THINK ABOUT

Can you write down ten sentences to do with staying healthy? Try to include phrases about eating habits as well as about an active lifestyle (including what to avoid in order to stay fit and healthy). You might also want to include phrases in different tenses. Try to mention the following:
- What you do to keep healthy at the moment (present tense)
- What you used to do (imperfect tense)
- What you will do in future (future tense)
- What you would do if you had more time (conditional tense)

ONLINE TEST

Take the 'La vida sana' test online at www. brightredbooks.net/ N5Spanish

LIFESTYLE-RELATED ILLNESSES – ENFERMEDADES RELACIONADAS CON EL ESTILO DE VIDA

We have looked at ways of staying healthy. Now we are going to learn to talk about unhealthy lifestyles. In this section, we will look at why people choose to smoke, drink alcohol or take drugs and what the consequences are.

BRAINSTORMING VOCABULARY

There are many illnesses that are caused by unhealthy lifestyles. Can you think of any lifestyle choices that could cause different illnesses? There are some words to help you get started in the diagram.

GENERAL VOCABULARY

Here is some general vocabulary that is useful to know. Cover the English meanings and 'traffic light' the vocabulary you already know (see page 8 to find out how to do this). Then focus on the vocabulary you don't know and learn it.

el tabaquismo	smoking
fumar cigarrillos	to smoke cigarettes
consumir alcohol	to consume alcohol
probar el alcohol	to try alcohol
ser perjudicial/dañino para la salud	to be harmful to your health
tomar drogas	to take drugs
drogarse	to take drugs
la dependencia/la adicción	addiction
la drogodependencia	drug addiction

ACTIVITY: Smoking and alcohol – El tabaco y el alcohol

You might want to think about why people choose to make certain lifestyle choices. Read and listen to the phrases below. First, decide if the person talking smokes or drinks alcohol or doesn't smoke or drink alcohol. Then try to work out why, looking up any words you don't know in the dictionary. After translating the phrases into English, choose which ones apply to you and memorise them. These can be used in your Performance.

Listening to the phrases online will help you with the pronunciation:

- No bebo alcohol porque no es bueno para la salud.
- Bebo alcohol porque me da confianza en mí mismo(a).
- No fumo porque el tabaco es muy caro.
- Bebo alcohol porque quiero escaparme de las preocupaciones de todos los días.
- Nunca fumo porque es perjudicial para la salud.
- Nunca bebo alcohol porque tiene un efecto negativo sobre el comportamiento.
- Bebo alcohol porque no quiero ser diferente a mis amigos.
- No bebo alcohol porque mis padres no confiarían en mí nunca más.
- Fumo porque me ayuda a relajarme.
- Bebo alcohol porque todos mis amigos beben alcohol.

DON'T FORGET

To work out who doesn't smoke or drink alcohol, you need to look out for negative words. Look back to page 9 to revise the different negatives in Spanish.

 contd

- Fumo porque es un hábito y es mi decisión.
- Bebo alcohol porque me ayuda a sentirme más cómodo(a).
- No fumo porque hay un riesgo de dependencia.
- No bebo alcohol porque mis padres se enojarían conmigo.
- Fumo porque me hace parecer más interesante.
- Incluso cuando estoy rodeado(a) de personas que fuman, no tengo ganas de fumar porque es peligroso para la salud.
- Todos mis problemas desaparecen cuando bebo alcohol.
- No fumo nunca porque tengo miedo de que no pueda parar.
- Fumo porque me relaja cuando estoy estresado(a).
- No bebo alcohol porque no me gusta el sabor y no fumo porque me marea.

DON'T FORGET

You will notice how *tengo ganas* and *tengo miedo* are used in some sentences. Look back to page 19 to revise *tener* phrases.

ACTIVITY: Why do people smoke or drink alcohol? – ¿Por qué la gente fuma o bebe alcohol?

Listen to the following three people talk about their lifestyles. Fill in the blanks using the words below.

Adrián

Yo quiero ser como mis _____, por eso fumo. Todos mis amigos _____ cigarrillos, así que estoy siempre rodeado de personas que fuman. Pienso que nos hace ser _____. Es mi decisión y estoy _____ de fumar. Ciertamente, yo diría que fumar me _____ a relajarme. Sé que hay _____ como el cáncer, pero no quiero dejarlo.

> amigos   contento   fuman   ayuda   interesantes   riesgos

Nuría

Yo bebo _____ desde hace dos años. Mis padres me dejan beber _____ de vino de vez en cuando. Cuando salgo con mis amigos, bebo alcohol porque me da más _____ en mí misma. Es verdad que la mayoría de mis amigos beben alcohol _____ y algunos beben demasiado. Lo que no me gusta es cuando están _____ porque el alcohol tiene un efecto muy negativo sobre el _____, que puede ser realmente vergonzoso.

> confianza   borrachos   comportamiento   alcohol   un vaso   regularmente

Juan Luis

Hace tres semanas, salí con mis amigos el viernes por la noche. Uno de mis amigos me_____ cannabis pero yo lo rechacé. A veces, bebo alcohol y fumo, pero nunca he tomado _____. Creo que son peligrosas porque si las _____ puedes volverte _____. Sé que si te drogas, puedes tener sensación de miedo, fatiga y pérdida de sueño. Lo más grave es que si sufres una _____ de droga, puedes morir. Además, si mis padres supieran que he probado el cannabis, ellos se _____ y no me darían libertad nunca más

> sobredosis   drogas   enojarían   pruebas   dependiente   ofreció

.

THINGS TO DO AND THINK ABOUT

Are there any phrases from these activities that you could use or that you could adapt? Jot down the phrases that apply to you and learn them as you may wish to use them for your Performance.

ONLINE

For an extra activity on lifestyle-related illnesses, head to www.brightredbooks. net/N5Spanish

VIDEO LINK

Watch the clip 'Enfermedades cardiovasculares' at www. brightredbooks.net/ N5Spanish

ONLINE TEST

Take the test 'Las enfermedades' at www. brightredbooks.net/ N5Spanish

DON'T FORGET

Desde hace means 'since' or 'for' and when used with a present tense verb it means you 'have been doing' that action for a certain length of time, for example *Juego al fútbol desde hace dos años* means 'I have been playing football for two years'. *Hace* followed by a time phrase, means 'ago' for example *hace dos semanas* means 'two weeks ago'.

DON'T FORGET

Algunos means 'some of them'.

TELEVISION – LA TELEVISIÓN

In this section you will learn to describe what you watch on TV.

USEFUL VOCABULARY

Here is some useful vocabulary to revise what we watch on TV. Match the Spanish vocabulary to the correct image. Try to work out what the Spanish vocabulary means by making links to English vocabulary, for example *una comedia* is 'a comedy' in English.

el telediario/las noticias/los informativos	una película de aventuras
los documentales (de naturaleza/historia …)	una película de guerra
los programas de deportes/de música	una película de ciencia ficción
los dibujos animados	una película policíaca
las telenovelas/los culebrones	una película de espías
los concursos	una película dramática
la publicidad/los anuncios	una película de terror/miedo
el pronóstico del tiempo/el parte meteorológico	una película romántica/de amor
un western	una película de acción
una comedia	una película de suspense

THINGS TO DO AND THINK ABOUT

Want to see how you did? Get the answers at the Bright Red Digital Zone online at www.brightredbooks.net/N5Spanish

 VIDEO LINK

For more on TV, watch Gary Lineker present *Match of the Day* in Spanish at www.brightredbooks.net

WATCHING TV – VIENDO LA TELE

As well as saying what you watch on TV, it would be good to be able to say how long you spend watching TV and what you enjoy watching, with reasons for your opinions.

 ACTIVITY OPINIONS OF DIFFERENT PROGRAMMES – OPINIONES SOBRE DIFERENTES PROGRAMAS

Listen to the following text and fill in the blanks using the words below. Read the text first and try to predict what you might hear, using the context as a basis for your prediction. Look up any new words in the dictionary before you start.

Sabrina

Yo paso cerca de dos horas al día delante de la pequeña _____. Me gusta ver las _____ y las comedias. Las encuentro _____ y para mí, es un buen medio para _____ porque no puedo concentrarme demasiado.

> pantalla   relajarme   telenovelas   divertidas

Ana

Yo no paso mucho tiempo viendo la tele, porque es una _____ de tiempo. Hay muchos jóvenes que ven la tele _____ y eso no es bueno para la salud. Si veo la tele, prefiero ver los _____ y los programas que me educan y me _____.

> informan   pérdida   documentales   sin parar

Carlos

Normalmente, no tengo suficiente tiempo para ver la tele durante la _____ porque tengo demasiados deberes. El viernes por la noche, me encanta ver películas _____ y películas de terror con mis amigos porque las encuentro _____. El sábado por la noche, a mi familia y a mí nos gusta ver los _____. Pienso que son graciosos y a veces hay preguntas difíciles, por lo que podemos aprender cosas.

> semana   emocionantes   concursos   policíacas

Roberto

Yo veo las noticias y el _____ _____ en la tele, así que me paso una hora delante de la pequeña pantalla. Creo que la tele es un buen medio de _____ y de descubrir lo que ocurre en el _____. Lo que está bien es que podemos ver las imágenes en directo, así que es más _____ que la radio.

> parte meteorológico   mundo   sorprendente   comunicación

Celia

Yo paso la mayor parte de mi tiempo libre viendo la tele. Mi madre dice que estoy _____ a la tele-realidad. Mi programa favorito se llama 'Top Chef' y nunca me _____ un episodio. Mi madre cree que es un programa superficial y _____. Ella me anima a hacer otras cosas más activas porque tiene miedo de que la tele me vuelva _____.

> tonto   enganchada   pierdo   perezosa

PRECEDING DIRECT OBJECTS

You will notice *lo encuentro, la encuentro, los/las encuentro* ... appear in some of the reading and listening texts. In these phrases, *lo, la, los, las* are known as **preceding direct objects.** Can you guess what they mean from the contexts?

Look at the examples and their translations and work out the grammar rule:

a   Me encanta el deporte. Lo veo en la tele todos los días.
    I love sport. I watch it on TV every day.

b   Me encanta mi falda. La llevo a menudo.
    I love my skirt. I often wear it.

c   No me gustan mis vecinos. ¡Los detesto!
    I don't like my neighbours. I hate them!

Lo and *la* are translated as 'it' and *los/las* are translated as 'them'. The preceding direct object must agree with the noun it refers to in terms of gender and number.

DON'T FORGET

No ... nunca is a negative phrase. Refer to page 9 to revise negatives. Negatives usually sandwich the verb. When using a preceding direct object, the negatives sandwich both the preceding direct object and the verb, for example: *Yo no la veo nunca.* – I never watch it.

ACTIVITY

Complete the following sentences by filling in the gap using the correct preceding direct object. (*lo/la/los/las*)

Me gustan los westerns. _____ veo a menudo.

Me encantan las comedias. _____ veo durante los fines de semana.

No me gustan los documentales . _____ veo raramente.

Odio el fútbol, pero _____ veo a veces.

Me gusta el pronóstico metereológico, por eso _____ veo todos los días.

No me gustan las películas policíacas. Nunca _____ veo.

VIDEO LINK

Check out the interview with TV news reporters at www.brightredbooks.net/N5Spanish

THINGS TO DO AND THINK ABOUT

Now write a paragraph about how much time you spend watching TV, what you watch on TV and why. Refer back to the section on opinion phrases on page 25 and try to include them. You may wish to use this as part of your Performance if you talk about what you do during your free time. You could include:

- your favourite TV programme and why

- when you watch TV

- with whom you watch TV.

ONLINE TEST

Try the 'Watching TV – Viendo la televisión' test online at www.brightredbooks.net/N5Spanish

REALITY TV – LA TELERREALIDAD

Reality TV shows have become very popular amongst young people. What do you think are the advantages and disadvantages of reality TV?

 **ACTIVITY:** For or against reality TV – A favor o en contra de la telerrealidad

Read the conversation between Matías y Lucía and answer the questions below. Before you do so, here are some tips for how to approach a reading text as part of the Unit and Course assessments.

- Start by reading the background information, as this will tell you what the text is about.

- Read the questions carefully.

- The answers usually come in the same order as the questions. These might also give you an idea of what the text is about.

- Pick out key words from the questions and use these to predict key words that you might see in the text.

- Look at the number of marks given for each question so you know how much information to give in your answers.

- When you read a word that you don't understand, try to make links with English words, refer to the glossary or use your dictionary to look up what they mean.

Matías y Lucía

M Hola Lucía, ¿viste un programa que se llama 'Secret Story' ayer por la noche? Estuvo genial. Me hizo reír mucho y lo encontré realmente divertido.

L No, detesto los programas de telerrealidad. La telerrealidad se ha vuelto más popular en estos últimos años. No aporta nada útil a la sociedad. Además, es difícil evitar los programas de telerrealidad, porque hay demasiados.

M No estoy de acuerdo. Los telespectadores lo encuentran fascinante. Por supuesto, mis padres dicen que estoy enganchado. A mi parecer, se trata de un concurso donde la gente quiere ganar mucho dinero o hacerse famosa. Les gustaría hacer realidad sus sueños, como por ejemplo convertirse en un cantante famoso, y de vez en cuando hay personas con mucho talento. A menudo es gente normal la que participa en los programas de telerrealidad. Yo siempre voto por los participantes que más me gustan.

contd

L ¿Hablas en serio? No te das cuenta de que es totalmente falso, ¡no es la realidad! Lo que no me gusta, es que a veces, los candidatos hacen cosas chocantes y desagradables. Pienso que la telerrealidad es una mala influencia sobre los jóvenes. Los jóvenes creen que no tienen por qué esforzarse en el instituto, ya que pueden hacerse ricos rápidamente gracias a los programas de telerrealidad. Tienen la impresión de que es suficiente participar en un programa de telerrealidad para ser famosos y ricos.

M Para mí, lo más interesante es observar la vida de las personas y cómo se relacionan con los otros. En mi opinión, tenemos miedo de comprender la verdadera naturaleza humana viendo ese tipo de programas. Lo que más me gusta, es que esos programas me dan la esperanza de que mi vida puede cambiar fácilmente también. Quizás me inscriba en la próxima edición de 'Secret Story'.

Questions

1 Why did Matías enjoy watching the programme 'Secret Story'? (2)

2 How does Lucía describe reality TV? (2)

3 Why does she think it's difficult to escape reality TV programmes? (1)

4 What does Matías say the programmes are about? (1)

5 What does Matías always do? (1)

6 What does Lucía not like and why? (1)

7 What does Lucía say about reality TV and young people? (3)

8 According to Lucía, what do young people believe? (2)

9 Who does Lucía say deserves publicity and big prizes? (1)

10 What does Matías find interesting about these programmes? (2)

THINGS TO DO AND THINK ABOUT

Using the text, pick out some phrases that reflect how you feel about reality TV. Write a paragraph on reality TV. Don't forget to use the opinion phrases and **conjunctions**. You may wish to use this paragraph as part of your Performance.

EXAMPLE

Creo que la telerrealidad es bastante interesante, porque muestra cómo son las personas realmente.

ONLINE

Check out the BrightRED Digital Zone for the answers to all the activities in this section: www.brightredbooks.net/N5Spanish

DON'T FORGET

When giving your opinion on something, always try to give a reason, introducing it with *porque* or *para* + infinitive. Example: Creo que tener un coche es muy útil para viajar.

VIDEO LINK

Watch some Spanish TV online by following the link at www.brightredbooks.net/N5Spanish

ONLINE TEST

Take the 'Reality TV – La telerrealidad' test online at www.brightredbooks.net/N5Spanish

TECHNOLOGY – LA TECNOLOGÍA

Technology has a huge part to play in our daily lives, from using your mobile phone to using the internet to shop for clothes. How many different forms of technology do you use regularly? Here are a few ideas to help you get started:

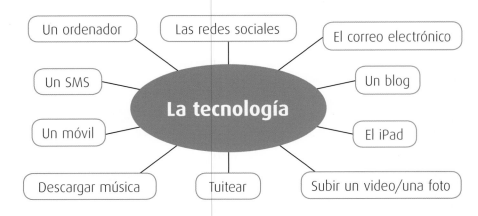

Un ordenador — Las redes sociales — El correo electrónico — Un SMS — **La tecnología** — Un blog — Un móvil — El iPad — Descargar música — Tuitear — Subir un video/una foto

ACTIVITY: Use of technology – El uso de la tecnología

It would be useful to be able to say how you use technology. Read the following phrases, put them into the first person and translate them into English. The first one has been put into the first person for you.

Listen to the phrases online to help you with the pronunciation.

- Enviar SMS/mensajes de texto a amigos con el móvil – Envío SMS/mensajes de texto a mis amigos con mi móvil.
- Reservar en línea/internet entradas para conciertos.
- Descargar películas y música.
- Buscar información para hacer los deberes.
- Hacer fotos con el móvil.
- Comprar libros por internet.
- Navegar por internet para encontrar información.
- Enviar correos electrónicos/emails.
- Utilizar internet para escuchar música y ver películas/ver la tele.
- Hacer la compra por internet/en línea.
- Estar en contacto con familiares que están en el extranjero gracias a internet.
- Sacar dinero de los cajeros automáticos.
- Comprar billetes de avión y reservar un hotel para las vacaciones por internet.
- Jugar a videojuegos en línea.

DON'T FORGET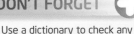

Use a dictionary to check any verbs that you are unfamiliar with.

 **ACTIVITY:** Advantages and disadvantages of technology – Las ventajas y los inconvenientes de la tecnología

There are many advantages and disadvantages of using technology.

First, read the following phrases and try to work out what they mean before listening to the audio track.

Use a dictionary to look up any unfamiliar vocabulary.

Then listen to the phrases online and put them under the correct heading of either *Ventajas* or *Inconvenientes*.

Finally, note down the reason(s) why they are advantages or disadvantages.

Transcript

1 La vida diaria es más fácil gracias a la tecnología. No sé qué haría sin mi (teléfono) móvil. Puedo estar en contacto con mis amigos y mis padres desde cualquier sitio.

2 A mi parecer, tener un buen móvil cuesta muy caro y puede hacer que la gente se vuelva más asocial. Además, el uso de los teléfonos móviles puede ser peligroso para la salud. Los móviles no son lo mío.

3 A mí me encanta el mundo virtual. Soy un verdadero internauta y hago todo a través de internet. Me compro ropa y descargo música y películas en línea, que es menos caro que comprar CDs y DVDs.

4 Para mí, la tecnología es maravillosa. Mi página web preferida es Facebook porque puedo comunicarme con mis amigos. Es muy rápido y se pueden ver fotos de amigos al instante. También me gusta Twitter, porque puedo seguir a mis amigos y a personas famosas.

5 Pienso que las comunidades virtuales pueden ser peligrosas porque podemos conocer a gente extraña cuando chateamos en línea. Hay gente amenazante que se oculta detrás de las pantallas.

6 Paso horas buscando productos en línea porque hay más opciones en internet que en las tiendas. Además puedo comparar los precios y comprar los productos más baratos.

7 Soy tecnófobo. Odio los ordenadores porque son complicados. No entiendo el lenguaje tecnológico.

8 Existen peligros en internet. Los padres se preocupan por la seguridad de sus hijos porque los jóvenes pueden ser víctimas del acoso por internet.

9 Dependemos mucho de nuestros móviles y de hecho, algunos dicen que no podrían sobrevivir sin su móvil. Enviamos SMS y correos electrónicos, vemos la tele, hablamos con amigos, leemos libros, navegamos por la red, jugamos a videojuegos y escuchamos música. Pasamos demasiado tiempo utilizando nuestros móviles y en consecuencia, hay menos comunicación entre las personas.

10 Lo que más me gusta es que puedo escuchar música en mi iPod sin molestar a nadie. También puedo leer libros de todo tipo en la misma pantalla con mi Kindle, que está genial.

 THINGS TO DO AND THINK ABOUT

Choose six phrases to describe how you use technology. Try to include:

- Three advantages of using technology.
- Three disadvantages of using technology.

You may wish to learn them for your Performance, and you could also use them as part of your writing about leisure and hobbies.

 ONLINE

Head to www.brightredbooks.net for a further activity on the internet.

 VIDEO LINK

For more on technology, watch the clip at www.brightredbooks.net/N5Spanish

 ONLINE TEST

Why not try the 'Technology – La tecnología' test at www.brightredbooks.net/N5Spanish?

YOUR HOME AREA AS A TOURIST AREA – LA ZONA DONDE VIVES COMO LUGAR TURÍSTICO

In this section you will learn to describe why tourists might come to your home area. You will revise how to say where you live and then learn to say what is in your town that tourists might want to come and see.

WHERE DO YOU LIVE? – ¿DÓNDE VIVES?

Let's start off by saying where in Scotland you live:

Vivo en …, en Escocia.

Grammar

To say that you live in a town and in a country, you need to know the following:

Vivo en + name of place: Glasgow/Madrid/Escocia/España …
Vivo en los/las + plural country: los Estados Unidos …

Now try to fill in the blanks with the correct phrase: *en, en los, en las.* Use the dictionary to find out the gender of the country.

Vivo __ Edimburgo.
Vivo __ Países Bajos.
Vivo __ España.
Vivo __ Emiratos Árabes Unidos.

Let's look at the points of the compass to say where in Scotland you live. Can you complete the points of the compass?

Note

The cardinal points are always written in lower case, except if they are part of a proper name, when they are capitalised. Example: Vivo en el norte de España; Vivo en América del Sur.

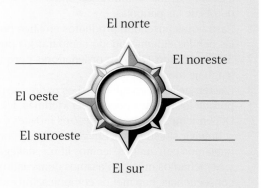

El norte

_____ El noreste

El oeste

El suroeste _____

El sur

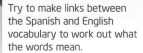 ACTIVITY

Do you live in a city or a town or in the countryside? Match the Spanish to the English and use a dictionary to look up any unfamiliar vocabulary.

en el campo	at the seaside
en la montaña	in a town
al lado del mar	in the outskirts
en una gran ciudad	in the mountains
en un pueblo	in the town centre
en el centro de la ciudad	in a city
en las afueras	in a village
en una ciudad	in the countryside

Now complete the sentences about where you live:

Vivo en … (name of place)
Mi ciudad/pueblo se encuentra en el … de Escocia. (location)
Vivo en … (town, countryside, etc.)

⚙ ACTIVITY: Describe your area – Describe tu barrio

It would be useful to be able to describe the area in which you live. Can you think of any adjectives that you could use to describe your home area? Here are a few to start you off. Look up any words you are not familiar with in the dictionary. Then put the adjectives under the headings: positivo/negativo.

- agradable
- animado(a)
- antiguo(a)
- bonito(a)
- contaminado(a)
- divertido(a)
- histórico(a)
- industrial
- limpio(a)
- magnífico(a)
- moderno(a)
- pintoresco(a)
- tranquilo(a)
- turístico(a)

⚙ ACTIVITY: My home town

Listen to the following texts online and fill in the blanks using the words in the box below. Read the text first to get the gist of what it is about and try to predict what you are going to hear.

1 Vivo en Aberdeen. Es una _____ _____ que se encuentra en el _____de Escocia. Creo que es una ciudad_____, dinámica y _____.

2 Yo vivo en West Linton. Es un _____ _____ que está situado cerca de Edimburgo en el _____ de Escocia. Creo que es un pueblo histórico, _____ y pintoresco.

3 Vivo en Girvan. Es una ciudad mediana que se encuentra __ ____ __ ___ en el _____ de Escocia. Pienso que es una ciudad _____, bonita y _____.

> al borde del mar   pequeño pueblo   turístico   industrial   limpia
> gran ciudad   animada   noreste   centro   suroeste   tranquila

▶ VIDEO LINK

To investigate this further, watch the clip 'El País Vasco – the Basque Country' at www.brightredbooks.net/N5Spanish

✓ ONLINE TEST

Take the 'Your home area as a tourist area – La zona donde vives como lugar turístico' test online at www.brightredbooks.net/N5Spanish

⚙ THINGS TO DO AND THINK ABOUT

Can you write a short paragraph to describe exactly where you live and what it is like? Try to include:

- The name of the place.
- The location.
- A brief description.
- Positive and negative things about the place.

Use the language in this section to help you. You may wish to use this as part of your writing and Performance.

A TOURIST TOWN – UNA CIUDAD TURÍSTICA

Can you think of what tourists visiting your home area might like to do? Think about the following:

¿Qué se puede hacer en tu ciudad? What can you do in your town?

ACTIVITY: My town – Mi ciudad

Read the following texts and answer the questions. You should look for key words and verbs that will help you to identify why their home area is a good place for tourists to visit. Try to give as much information as possible in your answers.

Felipe

Vivo en una ciudad pequeña y pintoresca. En verano hay muchos turistas que visitan mi ciudad porque se encuentra al lado del mar. Se puede caminar por la playa y pasear por la ciudad para ver los bonitos edificios, además puedes ir de compras, porque hay un centro comercial. La playa es ideal para los jóvenes activos a los que les gusten los deportes acuáticos. Este año se celebra un campeonato de piragüismo y también una competición de buceo a pulmón. Además, se pueden alquilar barcos, que es realmente divertido. Hay albergues juveniles donde poder alojarse durante la estancia. Yo siempre voy allí con mis amigos algún fin de semana de verano. También hay pequeños restaurantes típicos que son muy populares, porque tienen una comida deliciosa. En resumen, ¡mi ciudad es perfecta!

1 Where does Felipe live? Give two details. (2)
2 Name any three things that tourists can do when they visit his town in summer. (3)
3 What kind of sports can young people practise there? (1)
4 Where can they stay in the town? (1)
5 What does he say is popular and why? (2)

Sabrina

Mi ciudad es bastante grande y muy animada. Es un conocido destino turístico porque hay muchas cosas que hacer y que ver. Ante todo, se puede visitar un antiguo castillo, las ruinas romanas o un parque arqueológico. Si te gusta la historia, o las obras de arte, hay una gran variedad de museos y de galerías donde puedes pasar horas. A mí me gusta ir allí con mis amigas cuando hay una nueva exposición. Por la tarde, se pueden ver espectáculos de teatro o se puede asistir a conciertos. La actividad más popular entre

contd

los turistas es un recorrido por la ciudad a bordo de un autobús turístico. Pienso que mi ciudad es muy cultural y hay entretenimiento para todas las edades. Por ejemplo, para los niños hay una bolera, una pista de patinaje y un gran parque público. Además, hay muchos hoteles de cuatro y cinco estrellas y apartamentos de lujo que se pueden alquilar.

1 Where does Sabrina live? (1)
2 Why is it a well-known tourist destination? (1)
3 Name three places that you can visit there. (3)
4 What can you do in the evening? (2)
5 What is the most popular activity amongst tourists? (1)
6 What three places does Sabrina say would be good for children? (3)
7 Where can tourists stay? (2)

Juan Luis

Mi pueblo se encuentra en la montaña. Es cierto que es bastante pequeño, pero es conocido entre los turistas gracias al bellísimo paisaje que lo rodea. Si te gusta practicar senderismo, mi pueblo es el entorno ideal. Además, en invierno, cuando nieva, me encanta subir a las montañas a practicar esquí. Tengo suerte de vivir aquí porque el esquí es mi deporte favorito. Si quieres pasar la noche aquí, puedes alojarte en un pequeño hotel de tres estrellas que está situado en la calle principal. Puedes comer algo en los bares y hay también un restaurante tradicional que ha ganado muchos premios. Desafortunadamente, lo que no me gusta es que no hay muchas cosas que hacer por las tardes porque no hay cine o teatro. Sin embargo, en verano hay gente que viene de otros países para ir a los festivales y a las fiestas de música tradicional que hay cerca de mi pueblo, lo que está genial.

1 Where does Juan Luis live? (1)
2 What can you do in the area? (2)
3 Where can you stay? (1)
4 Where can you eat? (2)
5 What does he not like about where he lives? (1)
6 What happens in the summer? (2)

Clara

Vivo en las afueras de una gran ciudad dinámica y multicultural. Lo que más me gusta es que hay muchos turistas que visitan mi ciudad durante todo el año y hay un ambiente animado. A los turistas les gusta ir de tiendas, comprar recuerdos y probar los platos tradicionales en buenos restaurantes. También hay muchas atracciones turísticas. Si quieres ver algo de la región, puedes visitar los lagos, las montañas y las destilerías escocesas. Además, aunque no hay una buena red de transporte público, te puedes desplazar fácilmente. Finalmente, hay una gran variedad de alojamientos, como hoteles, albergues juveniles y pensiones, donde puedes hospedarte.

1 Where does Clara live? (3)
2 What does she like the most about her town? (2)
3 Name any three things tourists can do in Clara's city. (3)
4 What can you visit in the region? (3)
5 What does she say about transport? (2)
6 Where can you stay? (3)

THINGS TO DO AND THINK ABOUT

Using the language in this unit, write a paragraph about what there is for tourists to do in your home area. Think about it in terms of:

- location
- activities
- accommodation
- eating out.

You can learn this and you may wish to use this as part of your Performance.

DON'T FORGET

For more activities look at the section on sports and hobbies on page 23.

DON'T FORGET

Hay un museo means 'there is a museum' and *no hay cine* means 'there isn't a cinema'.

ONLINE TEST

Take the 'A tourist town – una ciudad turística' test online at www.brightredbooks.net/N5Spanish

VIDEO LINK

Take a guided tour around Madrid by watching the clip 'Mi ciudad, Madrid' at www.brightredbooks.net/N5Spanish

TOWN AND COUNTRY – LA CIUDAD Y EL CAMPO 1

In this section, we will compare life in a town or city to life in the countryside. Can you think of any obvious differences between the different ways of life?

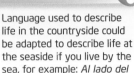

DON'T FORGET

Language used to describe life in the countryside could be adapted to describe life at the seaside if you live by the sea, for example: *Al lado del mar la vida es tranquila.*

DESCRIPTION OF THE TOWN AND THE COUNTRYSIDE – DESCRIPCIÓN DE LA CIUDAD Y DEL CAMPO

Have a look at the following adjectives. If there are any unfamiliar words, look up their meaning in the dictionary and then decide if the words best describe life in the town or in the countryside. Could they be used to describe both areas?

tranquilo(a)	cosmopolita	apacible	bonito(a)	contaminado(a)
relajante	estresante	animado(a)	aburrido(a)	divertido(a)
limpio(a)	ruidoso(a)	aislado(a)	caro(a)	sucio(a)

ONLINE

Head to www.brightredbooks.net/N5Spanish to see the answers and check how you got on!

ACTIVITY: The town – La ciudad

We will now focus on life in a town or a city.

Read the following phrases and try to work out what they mean by identifying familiar vocabulary. Translate the phrases into English using a bilingual dictionary. List the phrases as either advantages or disadvantages of living in a town/city.

- Es ruidoso(a).
- Hay mucha contaminación.
- Hay muchas cosas que hacer y que ver.
- No hay mucho que hacer.
- Se pueden visitar los monumentos históricos y las atracciones turísticas.
- Hay mucha basura en el suelo.
- Hay gran variedad de restaurantes.
- Hay demasiado tráfico.
- Se puede ir de tiendas en el centro de la ciudad.
- La vida nocturna está genial.
- Se puede ir a la discoteca por la noche.

- Hay muchas instalaciones donde hacer deporte.
- Hay demasiada gente.
- Los alquileres son caros.
- Te puedes desplazar fácilmente gracias a los medios de transporte público.
- No hay suficientes espacios verdes.
- Hay muchas diversiones para los jóvenes.
- La vida puede ser estresante.
- Te puedes beneficiar de la atmósfera cultural, como el teatro y los museos.
- No nos preocupa la vida de los vecinos.
- No nos sentimos seguros.

DON'T FORGET

Mucho(a) and *demasiado(a)* are useful words. *Muchas cosas* means 'a lot of things' and *demasiadas cosas* means 'too many things'.

DON'T FORGET

Cerca de and *lejos de* are **prepositions** and they tell us the position of something. Can you think of any other prepositions?

ACTIVITY: The countryside – El campo

We will now do the same exercise for the countryside.

- Estás aislado.
- No hay nada que hacer para los jóvenes.
- El paisaje es realmente bonito.
- Hace falta un coche para desplazarse.
- El estilo de vida es tranquilo.
- Todo el mundo se conoce.
- La vida puede ser aburrida y monótona.

- Hace falta ir a la ciudad para estudiar porque no hay institutos o universidades.
- No tenemos prisa.
- No hay distracciones.
- Hay muchos espacios verdes.
- Está bastante limpio.
- Es tranquilo y apacible.

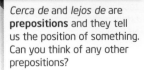 contd

- No hay comodidades cerca.
- El aire es puro porque hay menos contaminación.
- Se pueden dar largos paseos.
- Te puedes relajar.
- Vives cerca de la naturaleza.
- Hay menos posibilidades de encontrar un trabajo de oficina.

- Hay menos violencia.
- Vives lejos de tus amigos.
- Todo el mundo se entremete en la vida de los demás.
- Hay menos ruido.
- El transporte público no es bueno.

GRAMMAR: COMPARATIVES AND SUPERLATIVES

In this section, you have been comparing the town to the countryside.

In English we can compare things by putting 'er' at the end of an adjective (smaller, taller …) or by saying something is 'the ___-est' (e.g. the smallest, the tallest). In Spanish we use the following to compare things:

- más … (que)   more … (than)
- menos … (que)   less … (than)
- tan … (como)   just as … (as)
- el/la/los/las más … the most …
- el/la/los/las menos … the least …

EXAMPLE

Mi pueblo es pequeño.	My village is small.
Mi pueblo es más pequeño que tu ciudad.	My village is smaller than your city.
Mi pueblo es tan pequeño como tu ciudad.	My village is as small as your city.
Mi pueblo es el más pequeño.	My village is the smallest.
Tu ciudad es la más grande.	Your city is the biggest.

Be careful, there are some exceptions:

Adjective	Comparative	Superlative
bueno/a/os/as (good)	mejor/es (better)	el/la/los/las mejor/es (the best)
malo/a/os/as (bad)	peor/es (worse)	el/la/los/las peor/es (the worst)

EXAMPLE

El campo es mejor que la ciudad.	The countryside is better than the city.
La ciudad es la mejor opción.	The city is the best option.

ONLINE TEST

Take the 'Prepositions' test at www.brightredbooks.net/N5Spanish

THINGS TO DO AND THINK ABOUT

Now try to write a short paragraph about the advantages and disadvantages of living in the town and the countryside. How many of the phrases from the above sections can you remember? You may wish to use this as part of your Performance.

Example: En mi opinión, el campo es mejor que la ciudad porque hay menos contaminación. Sin embargo, la ciudad es menos aburrida que el campo porque siempre hay cosas que hacer.

VIDEO LINK

Check out the clip 'Holiday destinations' at www.brightredbooks.net/N5Spanish

TOWN AND COUNTRY – LA CIUDAD Y EL CAMPO 2

DON'T FORGET

The adjective must agree with the gender and number of the noun that it is describing.

VIDEO LINK

Have a look at 'Living in Barcelona' at www.brightredbooks.net/N5Spanish

ONLINE TEST

Take the 'Town and country – La ciudad y el campo' test online at www.brightredbooks.net\N5Spanish

ONLINE

Head to www.brightredbooks.net/N5Spanish for a third text about life at the seaside.

 **ACTIVITY:** Comparative and superlative – Comparativo y superlativo

Try to translate the following sentences using the comparative and superlative.

1 The town is more fun than the countryside
2 The town is less boring than the countryside.
3 The town is the most fun.
4 The countryside is the most boring.
5 The town is the least boring.
6 The town is the best.
7 The countryside is the worst.

ACTIVITY: Town or countryside – La ciudad o el campo

Read the following two texts and answer the following questions:

1 Where did each person use to live?
2 What did they like about it?
3 Where do they live now?
4 What do they like about it?
5 Where would they prefer to live if they had the choice and why?

Carlota

Cuando era pequeña, vivía en el campo. Nos mudamos porque mi padre encontró un trabajo nuevo. Me gustaba la vida en el campo porque todo el mundo se conocía y teníamos mucha libertad. Podíamos jugar durante horas cuando hacía buen tiempo porque había muchos espacios verdes. Ahora vivimos en una gran ciudad. Lo que más me gusta es que todos mis amigos viven cerca de mi casa. Es fácil desplazarse y siempre hay cosas que hacer, como ir al cine o ir de tiendas al centro comercial. Si pudiera elegir, viviría en la ciudad porque la vida aquí es mucho más animada que en el campo. Además hay muchísimo entretenimiento para los jóvenes.

Bernardo

Ahora vivimos en el campo. Es cierto que la vida en el campo es ideal porque hay menos peligros y violencia, así que me siento seguro. Además, me gusta mucho vivir cerca de la naturaleza y pasar mi tiempo libre practicando senderismo. Cuando era pequeño vivía en la ciudad. Por un lado, la vida en la ciudad era buena porque podías desplazarte fácilmente y había un montón de distracciones. Por el contrario, había demasiada gente, demasiada contaminación y demasiado ruido. En resumen, viviría en el campo, porque me encanta la tranquilidad y el estilo de vida apacible.

KNOWLEDGE ABOUT LANGUAGE

What do you notice about the verbs in the three reading texts? Can you spot the different tenses that we have already learned?

Can you spot the verbs in the present tense? Refer to page 7 to revise the present tense.
Can you pick out verbs in the preterite? Refer to page 69 to revise the preterite.
Can you pick out verbs in the imperfect tense? See below to revise the imperfect tense.
What about the future and conditional tenses? Refer to page 86 to revise these tenses.

GRAMMAR: THE IMPERFECT TENSE – EL PRETÉRITO IMPERFECTO

Take another look at the sections which describe where each person used to live and see if you can work out a pattern. The tense used is called the imperfect tense or *pretérito imperfecto*.

We use the imperfect tense:

- to describe a past repeated action
- to describe what something or someone was like in the past
- to say what someone 'used to do'
- to describe an interrupted action in the past – to say what someone/something was doing when something else happened.

How do we form the imperfect tense?

1 Write down the infinitive: *hablar, vivir* ...
2 Now chop off the *-ar, -er* or *-ir* and add the imperfect endings to the infinitive:

subject	*-ar* **verb endings**	*-er* **verbs**/*ir* **verb endings**
yo	**-aba**	**-ía**
tú	**-abas**	**-ías**
él/ella/usted	**-aba**	**-ía**
nosotros/nosotras	**-ábamos**	**-íamos**
vosotros/vosotras	**-ábais**	**-íais**
ellos/ellas/ustedes	**-aban**	**-ían**

EXAMPLE

(yo) habl*aba*	I used to talk/was talking
(tú) habl*abas*	you used to talk/ were talking
(él/ella/usted) habl*aba*	he/she used to talk/ was talking
(nosotros/nosotras) habl*ábamos*	we used to talk/were talking
(vosotros/vosotras) habl*ábais*	you used to talk/were talking
(ellos/ellas/ustedes) habl*aban*	they used to talk/were talking

EXAMPLE

(yo) viv*ía*	I used to live/was living
(tú) viv*ías*	you used to live/were living
(él/ella/usted) viv*ía*	he/she used to live/was living
(nosotros/nosotras) viv*íamos*	we used to live/were living
(vosotros/vosotras) viv*íais*	you used to live/were living
(ellos/ellas/ustedes) viv*ían*	they used to live/were living

There are only three irregular verbs in the imperfect tense: *ser, ver* and *ir*.

	ser	ver	ir
yo	**era**	**veía**	**iba**
tú	**eras**	**veías**	**ibas**
él/ella/usted	**era**	**veía**	**iba**
nosotros/nosotras	**éramos**	**veíamos**	**íbamos**
vosotros/vosotras	**érais**	**veíais**	**íbais**
ellos/ellas/ustedes	**eran**	**veían**	**iban**

THINGS TO DO AND THINK ABOUT

- Make up a paragraph about where you used to live and what you liked or didn't like.
- Then describe where you live now. Give opinions about what you think of it and why.
- To finish, say where you would like to live.

This is your chance to show how good you are so try to use different tenses, time phrases, linking words, comparatives, superlatives and opinion phrases. You may wish to use this as part of your Performance.

DON'T FORGET

Look for time phrases to help you identify the different tenses, for example *ahora* indicates an action happening in the present tense while *más adelante* refers to actions happening in the future.

ONLINE

Head to www.brightredbooks. net/N5Spanish for more on the imperfect tense.

VIDEO LINK

Learn more vocabulary by watching the clip at www.brightredbooks.net/ N5Spanish

ENVIRONMENT – EL MEDIO AMBIENTE

Can you think of different ways that you can be environmentally friendly at home? Here are a few ideas to help you get started:

Reutilizar las bolsas de plástico

Utilizar productos ecológicos

Reciclar

El medio ambiente

Desplazarse a pie

Reducir los residuos

Apagar la luz

ACTIVITY: Problems with our environment – Los problemas del medio ambiente

Let's start off by looking at the environmental problems that we are faced with. Read the phrases and try to match each of the pictures at the side with the most appropriate phrase. Then translate each phrase into English. Can you work out what they mean by making links to English phrases to do with environmental problems? If there are any phrases you are unsure of, use a bilingual dictionary to look them up.

1   la deforestación
2   el calentamiento global y el cambio climático
3   la contaminación del aire a causa de los vehículos
4   el tráfico y los atascos
5   la sequía
6   la extinción de especies amenazadas
7   el efecto invernadero y el agujero en la capa de ozono
8   la lluvia ácida debido a las actividades industriales
9   los residuos
10 los envases
11 el despilfarro de energía
12 la contaminación del agua

ACTIVITY: Protecting the environment – La protección del medio ambiente

Read through the following ways to help to protect our environment and translate them into English. Then match them to the problems above.

1   Hay que utilizar gasolina sin plomo.
2   Hay que proteger a las especies amenazadas, por ejemplo a los animales que viven en los bosques tropicales.
3   Hay que ir andando o utilizar los transportes públicos.
4   Hay que plantar árboles.
5   Hay que limitar la utilización de CFC.
6   Debemos separar los residuos para reciclar el papel, el plástico y el vidrio.
7   Hay que reducir el consumo de agua, cerrar los grifos y ducharse en lugar de bañarse.
8   Hay que utilizar las energías renovables y reducir la producción de dióxido de carbono.

9   Hay que reducir los residuos y evitar el despilfarro.
10 Hay que evitar tirar basura al mar.
11 Hay que reducir las emisiones de las fábricas y el consumo de combustibles fósiles.
12 Hay que conservar la energía y utilizar más energías limpias y renovables, como la energía solar, la energía eólica o hidráulica.

ACTIVITY: Modal verbs – Los verbos modales

Have a go at the activity 'What can we do to protect the environment?' on the BrightRED Digital Zone. This will help you with the next exercise.

Following the listening activity, try to complete this task.
1   Look at the infinitives in the box below and work out what they mean.
2   Complete the sentences.
3   Try to translate the sentences – this will be good practice for Higher Spanish!

Only look at the text from the listening if you get stuck, otherwise use your common sense fill in the blanks with the appropriate verb.

1   Hay que _____ los materiales reciclables, como los periódicos, el vidrio y el plástico.
2   Debemos _____ papel reciclado y pilas recargables en el supermercado.
3   Deberíamos _____ las bolsas de plástico.
4   Podríamos _____ el consumo de agua.
5   Podemos _____ productos ecológicos en la casa.
6   Deberíamos _____ a pie o en transporte público.
7   Hay que _____ la luz cuando salimos de una habitación.
8   No deberíamos _____ energía.
9   Debemos _____ el medio ambiente.
10 En lugar de _____, hay que ducharse.

> comprar   bañarse   reducir   apagar   malgastar
>
> reciclar   desplazarnos   proteger   reutilizar   utilizar

ONLINE

Complete the listening activity, 'What can we do to protect the environment?', at www.brightredbooks.net

DON'T FORGET

Debemos and *deberíamos* come from the verb *deber*, meaning 'must', and *Podemos* and *podríamos* come from the verb *poder*, meaning 'can' or 'to be able to'. Modal verbs are always followed by the infinitive.

VIDEO LINK

Watch the clips 'Ecotourism in Costa Rica' at www.brightredbooks.net/N5Spanish

THINGS TO DO AND THINK ABOUT

Write a short essay about what you and your family do to help the environment. Try to use some of the opening sentences and conjunctions from the activity 'What can we do to protect the environment?' (www.brightredbooks.net/N5Spanish). This could be used as part of your Performance. You could structure it in the following way:

Introduction: What is your short essay about? Name a few environmental problems.
Voy a escribir sobre el tema del medio ambiente. Hoy en día hay problemas medioambientales como …

Paragraph 1: What environmental problems are there?
Es cierto que hay muchos problemas medioambientales. Por ejemplo, …

Paragraph 2: What should everyone do?
Hay que/No hay que/Debemos/No debemos/Deberíamos/No deberíamos/Podemos
(+ infinitive).

Paragraph 3: What you do:
Yo …/Mi familia …/Mis padres … (See the phrases used in the listening transcript from the activity 'What can we do to protect the environment?' on the Digital Zone).

Conclusion:
En resumen, es importante proteger nuestro planeta.

LEARNING

EDUCATION – LA ENSEÑANZA

In this chapter we will look at the context of learning. The topics we will cover include:

- Learning activities you enjoy.
- Learning activities you don't enjoy.
- Preparing for exams.
- Comparing education systems in Scotland to other systems.
- How to improve education systems.

REVISION – REVISIÓN

At this stage, it would be worth revising school subjects. How many can you remember off the top of your head?

 **ACTIVITY:** Learning activities – Las actividades de aprendizaje

Think about the range of activities you do in each subject. Can you work out what the following activities mean in English?

1 Aprender el vocabulario
2 Resolver problemas
3 Trabajar individualmente
4 Trabajar en grupo/en equipo
5 Trabajar en parejas
6 Trabajar en el ordenador
7 Copiar los datos del recuadro/de la tabla
8 Ver documentales
9 Leer
10 Buscar las palabras en el diccionario
11 Buscar información
12 Escribir redacciones
13 Crear
14 Diseñar
15 Hacer los deberes
16 Hacer presentaciones
17 Tocar instrumentos
18 Hacer actividades deportivas
19 Participar en los juegos
20 Escuchar al profesor
21 Hablar con los compañeros de clase
22 Estudiar aritmética y álgebra
23 Hacer trabajos manuales como el bricolaje
24 Cocinar
25 Aprender gramática
26 Aprender ortografía
27 Aprobar los exámenes (orales/escritos)
28 Hacer experimentos científicos

 **ACTIVITY:** Subjects and activities – Las asignaturas y las actividades

1 Write a list in Spanish of the subjects you are currently studying at school.

2 Beside each subject write at least one activity that you do in this subject. Try to put the infinitives into the *yo* form (refer to page 7 if you need to revise how to form the present tense). Look up the verb section in your dictionary to check any irregular verbs.

 **ACTIVITY:** What do you like doing at school/college or university? – ¿Qué te gusta hacer en el instituto/la universidad?

Now that you have decided which activities you do in different subjects, you will learn how to give your opinion on the different activities. Refer to page 25 to revise opinion phrases before you start this exercise.

 Listen to the following four people discussing what they like and dislike doing at school and complete the table below. Write as much as you can under each heading (you may need to use extra paper).

Name	Subject	Activities they enjoy	Reason	Activities they dislike	Reason
Federico					
Coral					
Ramón					
Ana					

 THINGS TO DO AND THINK ABOUT

Can you write about some of the learning activities you do at school? Try to include:

● Which activities you do in different subjects.

● Which activities you enjoy and why.

● Which activities you do not enjoy and why.

Don't forget to give reasons for your opinions. You may wish to use this as part of your Performance.

 DON'T FORGET

When giving your opinion in Spanish remember that phrases like *me gusta, me encanta, no me gusta, detesto* and *prefiero* are all followed by the verb in the infinitive. For example *me gusta trabajar* means 'I like to work' but often in English we translate it as 'I like working'.

 ONLINE TEST

Take the test 'School subjects – Las asignaturas' at www.brightredbooks.net/N5Spanish

 VIDEO LINK

Check out the clip 'A day in a Spanish secondary school' at www.brightredbooks.net/N5Spanish

PREPARING FOR EXAMS – PREPARÁNDOSE PARA LOS EXÁMENES 1

As you are using this book, it is likely you are preparing for your Spanish exams. In this section we will look at different types of exams and how best to prepare for them.

TO SIT EXAMS – PRESENTARSE A LOS EXÁMENES

Let's start by thinking about how you might introduce talking about your exams. We all strive to do well and, by getting good grades in your exams, you will have a lot of opportunities open to you. We will start by saying what exams you are sitting and that you need to work hard this year to succeed. Can you work out what the following phrases mean?

- Este año me presento a los exámenes de National 5.

- Estudio seis asignaturas, incluyendo matemáticas, inglés, español, historia, música y biología.

- Estoy preparando mis exámenes de National 5.

- Voy a presentarme a mis exámenes de National 5 a final de curso.

- Voy a aprobar mis exámenes este año porque tengo la intención de continuar mis estudios el año que viene.

- Si tengo buenas notas, podré encontrar un buen empleo en el futuro.

- Debo trabajar mucho para aprobar mis exámenes.

- Tengo que estudiar mucho para aprobar los exámenes, porque tengo ganas de terminar el instituto y encontrar un buen empleo.

At this point, you could link why you want to do well in your exams to your future plans. Refer to the section on future plans on page 72.

ACTIVITY: The exams – Los exámenes

Now look at the different types of tasks that you might have to do as part of your exams. Can you work out what they mean in English? You could try to guess which subject(s) each phrase refers to.

1 Tengo exámenes escritos y orales.

2 Tengo que presentarme a exámenes de comprensión auditiva.

3 Debo leer textos.

4 Debo hacer presentaciones.

5 Debo responder a preguntas.

6 Hay que escribir redacciones.

7 Hay que hacer experimentos.

8 Hay que estudiar aritmética.

9 Hay que preparar una comida.

10 Debo tocar la guitarra/debo cantar.

11 Debo diseñar imágenes.

12 Debo hacer trabajos manuales.

13 Hay que resolver problemas.

14 Hay que practicar deporte.

15 Hay que trabajar en el ordenador.

ACTIVITY: Preparation – La preparación

What preparation do you do for your different exams? Match the Spanish phrases to the English translations:

Asisto a clase	I learn useful words and definitions off by heart
Practico para el examen de español	I do research
Hago repaso en línea	I spend a lot of time doing revision at home
Utilizo páginas web para revisar en internet	I go to extra classes
Busco información	I attend lessons
Leo mis apuntes	I practise for the Spanish exam
Aprendo palabras y definiciones útiles de memoria	I do revision online
Paso mucho tiempo repasando en mi casa	I read my notes
Voy a clases complementarias	If there are things I don't understand, I ask my teacher to explain
Tengo un horario para repasar	I have a revision timetable
Si hay cosas que no entiendo, le pido a mi profesor que me las explique	I use websites to do revision on the internet

DON'T FORGET

Asistir a means 'to attend', not 'to assist'.

ONLINE TEST

To test your knowledge of more false friends try the test at www.brightredbooks.net/N5Spanish

VIDEO LINK

Check out the clip 'El instituto' at www.brightredbooks.net/N5Spanish

THINGS TO DO AND THINK ABOUT

Look back at the phrases above. Try to think of three further sentences in Spanish about things you do to prepare for exams. You could refer back to the sections on leisure and healthy living and use some phrases from there to help you out.

PREPARING FOR EXAMS – PREPARÁNDOSE PARA LOS EXÁMENES 2

 **ACTIVITY:** The pressure of exams – La presión de los exámenes

Read the following texts and then answer the questions below.

Benjamín

En este momento estoy estudiando para mis exámenes. Creo que hay mucha presión y mis padres siempre están encima de mí. Es realmente difícil porque no soy trabajador y prefiero pasar mi tiempo libre navegando por internet o jugando a videojuegos en línea. Para mí, es muy importante encontrar el equilibrio entre los estudios y el tiempo de ocio, pero mis padres no están de acuerdo. Dicen que debo estudiar durante horas sin hacer pausas, pero yo encuentro el repaso insoportable y realmente aburrido. Después de hacer los exámenes, tengo ganas de terminar el instituto y de encontrar un empleo. No tengo la intención de continuar mis estudios en el instituto.

Laura

Este año me estoy preparando para mis exámenes. Sé que es mi responsabilidad porque tengo la intención de continuar mis estudios en la universidad y por eso tengo que aprobar los exámenes. Eso puede ser estresante pero sé que es solo durante algunos meses. No salgo mucho con mis amigos porque me dedico a mis estudios. Sé que es importante dormir bien, hacer pausas y comer bien, porque nos podemos concentrar mejor si nos encontramos bien. Mis padres me apoyan y ellos saben que hago lo que puedo.

1 Who is not coping well with the pressure of exams?
2 Who is taking responsibility for their exams?
3 Who is working hard?
4 Who would prefer to be on the computer instead of studying?
5 Whose parents are very supportive?
6 Whose parents are putting them under a lot of pressure?
7 Who is not going to continue studying?
8 Who wants to go to university?
9 Who doesn't see their friends much?
10 Who is told to study for hours without taking a break?
11 Who thinks that being healthy will help them to concentrate?

contd

Now find the Spanish for the following in the texts:

1   There is a lot of pressure.
2   It's my responsibility.
3   My parents are always on my back.
4   I have to pass my exams.
5   I prefer spending my free time …
6   To find the balance between studies and leisure …
7   I find revision unbearable.
8   It can be stressful.
9   I devote myself to my studies.
10 I don't intend to continue.
11 You can concentrate better if you feel well.
12 I am doing what I can.

THINGS TO DO AND THINK ABOUT

There may be some phrases in the text that you might like to use in your Performance.

Write a paragraph about:

- Your ambitions to do well in your exams

- The exams you are working towards

- What exactly you have to do

- How you prepare for your exams

- Whether you think you are coping well with the pressure.

ONLINE TEST

Try the 'Preparing for exams' test at www.brightredbooks.net/N5Spanish

DON'T FORGET

Después de haber is known as the **perfect infinitive** and it is translated as 'after having done something' for example *después de haber aprobado mis exámenes* means 'after having passed my exams'. It is followed by the past participle.

VIDEO LINK

Watch the video 'School life' at www.brightredbooks.net/N5Spanish

ONLINE

Follow the link at www.brightredbooks.net/N5Spanish for more on this topic.

DIFFERENT EDUCATION SYSTEMS – LOS DISTINTOS SISTEMAS EDUCATIVOS

The Scottish education system is very different from systems in other countries.

VIDEO LINK

Watch the clip 'School life in the Sahara' at www.brightredbooks.net/N5Spanish

DON'T FORGET

Revise Spanish numbers regularly. In this topic about school, you need to recognize and understand different numbers in the context of time and the number of pupils at school.

ACTIVITY: The school system – El sistema educativo

Read the following texts about two young people talking about their school system and answer the questions in the table.

Sofía

Voy a un instituto de Madrid. Es un instituto mediano, con novecientos cincuenta alumnos. El edificio es moderno y está bien equipado. Voy al instituto en bicicleta. Las clases empiezan a las ocho y cinco y terminan a las tres menos diez. Hay siete clases al día y cada clase dura cincuenta minutos. Hay un recreo de media hora a las once menos cuarto. Durante el recreo, picamos algo en la cafetería del instituto. La comida es muy sana y hay mucha variedad. Después del instituto, vamos a casa y comemos en familia. Estudio ocho asignaturas, y mi asignatura preferida es el dibujo artístico. Hay veintisiete alumnos en mi clase y a veces hace falta ir a otras aulas, por ejemplo a los laboratorios y a las salas de informática. También hay bastantes actividades extraescolares, como un club de teatro, otro de lectura y un equipo de baloncesto. Me gustan los profesores en el instituto porque son comprensivos y pacientes. En el instituto no tenemos que llevar uniforme y eso me parece una mala idea. Prefiero llevar uniforme, porque es caro ir al instituto con ropa de moda diferente cada día. Lo que más me gusta es que puedo pasar tiempo con mis amigos. Hablamos y nos reímos durante el recreo. Por otra parte, no hay suficientes bancos en el patio del instituto y eso no me gusta.

Pedro

Mi instituto se encuentra en Bogotá, Colombia. Es un instituto grande con mil setecientos alumnos. Es un edificio viejo y anticuado. Voy al instituto caminando, así que me tengo que levantar muy temprano todos los días, porque las clases empiezan a las ocho en punto. Las clases terminan a las tres y veinte. Hay ocho clases al día y duran cuarenta y cinco minutos. Tenemos un recreo que dura veinte minutos y una hora para comer. Normalmente vuelvo a casa para comer porque en la cafetería del colegio la comida es muy cara. Estudio nueve asignaturas y mi asignatura favorita es la geografía. Hay treinta y cinco alumnos en mi clase y nos quedamos en la misma aula durante todo el día. Hay un campo de fútbol y una pista de baloncesto. En cuanto a las actividades extracurriculares, tenemos un club de ajedrez, un equipo de fútbol, otro de natación y un club de informática. Los profesores son muy accesibles y respetan a los alumnos. Las normas del instituto son muy estrictas, por ejemplo, no tenemos el derecho a utilizar celulares o a hablar durante las clases. Lo que más me gusta es que no hace falta llevar uniforme y eso es muy cómodo. Lo que no me gusta es que no hay suficientes computadores.

Questions	Sofía	Pedro	Elena (listening)
Where is the school?			
What size is it?			
How many pupils are there?			
What is the building like?			
How do they get to school?			
What time do lessons start and finish?			
How many classes do they have per day and how long does each class last?			
What time is lunch?			

contd

How long is the lunch break?			
Where do they eat lunch?			
What is their opinion of the canteen?			
How many subjects do they study?			
What is their favourite subject?			
How many pupils are there in their classes?			
What facilities are there?			
What are the extracurricular activities?			
What do they say about their teachers?			
Do they wear a uniform?			
What is their opinion of wearing a uniform?			
What do they like about school?			
What do they not like about school?			

⚙ ACTIVITY: Elena's School

Now that you have read about Sofia's and Pedro's schools, listen to Elena describe her school. Use the same table as before and complete as many details as possible by listening out for key words.

⚙ ACTIVITY: The school system in Scotland – El sistema educativo en Escocia

Now that you have read about different school systems in different Spanish speaking countries, it would also be a good idea to think about how these schools differ from Scottish schools. Listen to Manuel describing the school system in Scotland. Here are some tips:

- Read the information that you are required to find (the questions/the table) and underline key words.
- Think about the vocabulary that you might hear and predict the key words that you need to listen out for (*edificio/alumnos/comienzo/final/profesores* etc.).
- Put a star or a tick beside the questions that you didn't complete, so the second time you listen to the text, you know what questions and information to focus on.
- The third time you listen to the text should be your chance to fill in any remaining gaps and check that the answers you have written down are correct.
- Make sure you always check your answers carefully – do they actually answer the questions?
- Don't leave any blanks, do your best to make an intelligent guess!

Questions:

1 Where is the school that Manuel visited?
2 What size is it?
3 How many pupils are there in the school?
4 What is the building like?
5 When do classes start and finish?
6 What time is lunch?
7 What do most pupils do at lunch time?
8 How many subjects do pupils study?
9 How many pupils are in each class?
10 What does he say about pupils wearing uniform?
11 What does Manuel like about Scottish schools?
12 What does Manuel dislike about Scottish schools?

ONLINE TEST

Take the test on different education systems at www.brightredbooks.net/N5Spanish

THINGS TO DO AND THINK ABOUT

Using the reading and listening texts in this section as a guide for structure and content, write as much as you can about your school. You can select appropriate vocabulary from the reading texts and the listening transcripts, and change the key information to describe your school. Try to answer the same questions from the table for the first activity. You can use this text as part of your Performance.

IMPROVING EDUCATION SYSTEMS – MEJORANDO LOS SISTEMAS EDUCATIVOS

HOW CAN YOU IMPROVE YOUR EDUCATION SYSTEM? – ¿CÓMO SE PUEDE MEJORAR NUESTRO SISTEMA EDUCATIVO?

We have looked at the education systems in different countries. Was there anything that you liked about the other systems that you would like to happen in your school? Think about the following:

 **ACTIVITY:** My preferences at school – Mis preferencias en el instituto

Have a look at the following phrases, which describe some common complaints about schools and explain what the ideal situation would be. Translate them into English and try to match the complaints to the correct ideal situation.

Common complaints	Ideal situation
Las clases son aburridas.	Me gustaría llevar la ropa que quiera al instituto.
Creo que las asignaturas tradicionales son bastante monótonas.	Preferiría tener un recreo de media hora.
Las clases empiezan a las nueve.	Me gustaría tener más material deportivo.
No hay demasiadas actividades extraescolares.	Prefiero estar en una clase de veinte alumnos.
Las clases terminan a las tres y media.	Me gustaría tener dos horas para almorzar.
Tenemos cuarenta y cinco minutos para el almuerzo.	Me gustaría tener unas clases interesantes y divertidas.
Tenemos un recreo de quince minutos.	Me gustaría tener más variedad de actividades extraescolares.
La comida del comedor es demasiado cara y no hay mucha variedad.	Me gustaría estudiar asignaturas más modernas y dinámicas, como la danza.
No hay suficientes ordenadores.	Me gustaría tener más libertad en el instituto.
No hay suficiente material deportivo.	Me gustaría terminar a la una de la tarde.
La biblioteca es pequeña y no hay suficiente variedad de libros.	Me gustaría empezar a las once.
Hay 35 alumnos por clase.	Debería haber más deportes de equipo.
Los alumnos no tienen mucha libertad.	Prefiero los profesores relajados.
Hay que llevar un uniforme horrible.	Me gustaría tener más salas de informática en el instituto.
No tenemos que llevar uniforme.	Me gustaría tener profesores que no pongan deberes.
Solo hay clubs de deportes individuales.	El comedor debería tener platos más baratos y más variedad.
Mis profesores son muy severos.	Me gustaría tener una biblioteca grande con una gran variedad de libros.
Los profesores nos ponen muchos deberes.	Me gustaría llevar uniforme, porque iguala a todo el mundo.

ACTIVITY: The rules – El reglamento

Let's focus more closely on the rules in school that you would like to change and the reasons why. Listen to the following people talking about which rules they would like to change at their school and why. Fill in the gaps using the words in the boxes below. Here are some tips to help you complete this listening task:

- Read through the texts first, to get an idea of what the subject matter is, and use your dictionary to look up any new words you don't recognise.
- Try to predict what you might hear by guessing in advance what words might fit into the blanks.
- Listen to the text as many times as you need to, until all the gaps have been filled in.

Antonio

En mi opinión, mi instituto no es un _____ instituto. Hay demasiadas _____ y hay que seguirlas. Durante las clases debemos _____ al profesor y no podemos _____ o comer en el aula. Además, no tenemos derecho a utilizar el _____ en el instituto, incluso durante el recreo o a la hora del almuerzo. Creo que el reglamento no es _____.

| beber | buen | justo | móvil | escuchar | reglas |

Beatriz

En mi instituto hay que llevar uniforme. Algunos piensan que es una _____ idea porque todo el mundo _____ igual y entonces no hay _____. Yo pienso que el uniforme es una buena idea. No _____ caro y es mejor no remarcar las diferencias _____ entre los alumnos. Además, no se _____ tiempo decidiendo qué llevar puesto cada mañana.

| es | individualidad | pierde | sociales | parece | mala |

ACTIVITY EXTRACURRICULAR ACTIVITIES – ACTIVIDADES EXTRAESCOLARES

Take a look at the different extracurricular activities in the table. Try to translate them into English. Which ones do you already have in your school? Can you add any other extracurricular activities to the list?

coro	club de periodismo	equipo de fútbol	club de lectura
club de ajedrez	orquesta	club de teatro	taller de música
taller de diseño	club de fotografía	equipo de rugby	club de informática
club de natación	taller de baile	club de idiomas	equipo de baloncesto

THINGS TO DO AND THINK ABOUT

Now write a paragraph describing what happens at your school and what you would like to change. Use the phrases in this section to help you or try to make up your own. Think about:

- the school day: your subjects, teachers, school rules ...
- facilities: canteen, extra-curricular activities ...

Try to include a couple of phrases using the conditional tense. You may wish to use this paragraph as part of your Performance.

DON'T FORGET

Try to use the conditional tense or talk about your ideal school.

DON'T FORGET

The conditional tense is used to describe what something 'would be' or what someone 'would do'. Refer to page 86 to revise the conditional tense.

ONLINE

Have a look at the 'Education system in Spain' link to read about how the school system works in Spain and jot down anything you'd like to see in Scotland: www.brightredbooks.net/N5Spanish

ONLINE TEST

Take the 'Improving education systems' test at www.brightredbooks.net/N5Spanish

DIFFERENT JOBS – LOS DISTINTOS TRABAJOS

This chapter on employability is all about the world of work. We'll start by revising different types of jobs.

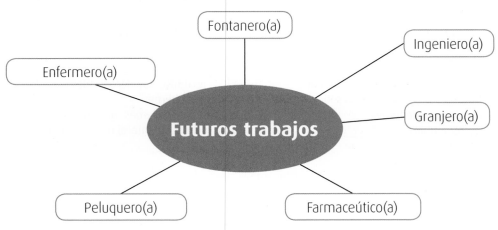

Fontanero(a)

Ingeniero(a)

Enfermero(a)

Futuros trabajos

Granjero(a)

Peluquero(a)

Farmacéutico(a)

 ACTIVITY: Where Do You Work? – ¿Dónde Trabajas?

Look at the following phrases about places of work. Can you match the phrases to the correct job?

Trabajo en un hospital.	Soy enfermero.
Trabajo en un instituto.	Soy vendedora.
Trabajo en un colegio de primaria.	Soy policía.
Trabajo en un restaurante.	Soy camarero.
Trabajo en un taller.	Soy secretaria.
Trabajo en una comisaría.	Soy maestro.
Trabajo en una oficina.	Soy profesora.
Trabajo en una tienda.	Soy mecánico.

 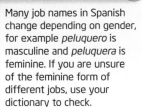

 **ACTIVITY:** Skills for different jobs – Cualidades necesarias para los distintos trabajos

Different jobs require different skills, for example to be a teacher you need to be patient, organised and have good communication skills.

Have a look at the following phrases about skills and match them to the jobs. Use your dictionary to work out the meaning of any unfamiliar vocabulary.

farmacéutico(a)   periodista   bombero(a)   recepcionista

1   Hay que ser trabajador(a) y estar en forma.
2   Debes estar motivado(a) y ser decidido(a).
3   Hay que ser organizado(a) y flexible.
4   Tiene que gustarte trabajar en equipo.
5   Hay que tener energía y entusiasmo.
6   Hay que tener buenas notas y una titulación.
7   Debes ser capaz de trabajar bajo presión.
8   Hay que tener conocimiento de ordenadores.
9   Debes tener una buena memoria.
10 Debes saber escribir a máquina muy rápido.
11 Es útil hablar otro idioma.

 **ACTIVITY:** Revision – Revisión

1   Choose three different jobs and write down in Spanish what skills you need for them using the vocabulary you have just learned.

2   Now translate the following paragraphs into English using all of the vocabulary from this section. Use a dictionary to help you work out the meaning of any unfamiliar language.

a   Me gustaría ser médico. Tengo que aprobar los exámenes y necesito sacar buenas notas. Para ser médico se debe tener paciencia, saber comunicarse bien con los enfermos y tener la capacidad de trabajar bajo presión.

b   Me encantaría ser músico. Necesitas ser creativo y tener mucho talento, entusiasmo y energía. Me gustaría saber hablar otro idioma porque sería útil para viajar por el mundo.

c   En el futuro me gustaría ser veterinaria. Tienes que ser trabajadora, educada y organizada. Hay que saber comunicarse con los demás y amar a los animales. Además, es importante tener una buena memoria.

d   En un futuro, me encantaría ser auxiliar de vuelo. Hay que estar en forma, ser sociable y educado. Me gustaría viajar alrededor del mundo y quizás vivir en el extranjero. Necesitas trabajar en equipo y tiene que gustarte el trabajo de cara al público.

 DON'T FORGET

Hay que/tienes que and *debes* are always followed by the infinitive. *Debes* comes from the modal verb *deber*, and *saber* is another modal verb meaning 'to know how to'. To revise modal verbs, look at pages 26-7.

VIDEO LINK

Check out the clip about the world of work: www.brightredbooks.net/N5Spanish

 THINGS TO DO AND THINK ABOUT

Using the vocabulary in this section choose a job that you would like to do in the future and write a paragraph about the qualities you need to have to do this job successfully. You will be able to add to this when we get to the section on future plans and may wish to use this as part of your Performance. You should also refer to the section on writing to help you.

EXAMPLE

En un futuro me gustaría ser piloto de avión. Hay que ser responsable y trabajar mucho. Me gustaría viajar por distintos países. Además, debes hablar varios idiomas.

PART-TIME JOBS – LOS TRABAJOS A TIEMPO PARCIAL 1

You might already have a part-time job or you might be considering getting one to earn some money. Let's brainstorm some of the jobs you could do. Can you add any others?

ACTIVITY: My part time job – Mi trabajo a tiempo parcial

Los trabajos a tiempo parcial

- Camarero(a)
- Vendedor(a)
- Cajero(a)
- Canguro
- Recepcionista

Read the following sentences and note down where each person works and what jobs they do.

1 Trabajo en una cafetería, soy camarero(a).

2 Trabajo en un hotel, soy recepcionista.

3 Trabajo en una tienda, soy vendedor(a).

4 Trabajo en un supermercado, soy cajero(a).

5 Cuido a los niños de mis vecinos, soy su canguro.

APPLYING FOR A PART-TIME JOB – SOLICITUD DE TRABAJO A TIEMPO PARCIAL

ONLINE

For further practice in reading and working out the meaning of job adverts, refer to the website links at www.brightredbooks.net/N5Spanish

If you are thinking of applying for a part-time job, it would be very useful to put together a CV. Use the links listed to help you write a CV in Spanish. Some of the vocabulary that you will need to write a CV can also be used in the Writing section of your exam. Refer to the chapter on writing (page 82 onwards) to help you.

You may also want to write a cover letter/email in Spanish.

ACTIVITY: Jobs adverts – Ofertas de empleo

Read the following job adverts and try to pick out some key points: what the job is, the hours, the pay and anything else you can understand. Then answer these questions:

1 Which job would you apply for and why?

2 Which job would you not apply for and why?

Anuncio 1

Puesto: Camarero(a)

¿Te gusta la comida? ¿Eres trabajador(a) y estás motivado(a)?

Te ofrecemos la posibilidad de trabajar como camarero(a) en nuestro pequeño restaurante familiar situado en las afueras de Barcelona. Debes tener más de 16 años. Ofrecemos un trabajo de diez horas a la semana, principalmente los lunes por la tarde y los fines de semana por la mañana.

Las comidas están incluidas en el salario, que es de siete euros por hora más propinas. Ocasionalmente se trabajará en turno de noche.

Si estás interesado(a), ponte en contacto con nosotros en este número: 06 56 89 76 20.

contd

Anuncio 2

Puesto: Peluquero(a) en prácticas

Ofrecemos prácticas profesionales en un salón de peluquería localizado en el centro de la ciudad.

Es una oportunidad ideal para adquirir las competencias necesarias para convertirse en peluquero(a). Debes ser educado(a), servicial y entusiasta. Hay que organizar las citas con los clientes, lavar el pelo de los clientes y trabajar en la caja.

No es necesaria experiencia previa. Se trabajará el sábado de nueve de la mañana a cinco de la tarde.

El salario es de seis euros y veinticinco céntimos por hora.

Si estás interesado(a) llama al 09 67 56 38 72.

Anuncio 3

Puesto: Jardinero(a)

¿Te gusta estar al aire libre? Se buscan jóvenes para trabajar en jardines públicos.

Debes tener entre 13 y 16 años y hay que ser enérgico(a), honesto(a) y puntual. Hay que regar las plantas y las flores y cuidar el estado de la tierra. Ofrecemos un trabajo diario de una hora después de clase y posibilidad de un par de horas más los fines de semana, (horarios a acordar).

Es necesario el permiso de los padres. Se puede trabajar cerca de casa y ganar treinta y cinco euros a la semana.

Para más información, interesados(as) llamad al 06 87 29 65 12.

THINGS TO DO AND THINK ABOUT

When applying for a job you will need to describe the skills/interests/experience you already have that are related to the job. Here are some phrases you could use:

– Me interesa el trabajo con gente/animales/ordenadores …
– I am very interested in working with people/animals/computers …

– Soy competente en el uso de las nuevas tecnologías/los idiomas …
– I am competent in the use of new technologies/languages …

– Me gustaría trabajar para obtener experiencia laboral.
– I would like to work in order to get work experience.

– Tengo experiencia en trabajos relacionados con …
– I have experience in jobs related to …

– Estoy dispuesto a trabajar mucho.   – I am willing to work hard.

– Tengo capacidad de liderazgo.   – I have leadership skills.

– Puedo trabajar en equipo.   – I work well within a team.

– Soy puntual, responsable, organizado(a), dinámico(a) …
– I am punctual, responsible, organized, dynamic …

 ONLINE TEST

Test how well you have learned about part-time jobs at www.brightredbooks.net/N5Spanish

PART-TIME JOBS – LOS TRABAJOS A TIEMPO PARCIAL 2

⚙ ACTIVITY: What do you do at work? – ¿Qué haces en el trabajo?

If you already have a part-time job, or for the sake of the Writing exam you are pretending to have a part-time job, you might want to say what your responsibilities and duties are at work.

Read the following phrases and decide which job is being described. Some phrases can be used for more than one job. Don't forget to use your dictionary to look up the meaning of any unfamiliar vocabulary. The jobs being described are:

recepcionista   cajero(a)   vendedor(a)   canguro   camarero(a)

1   Debo ordenar la ropa.
2   Hay que servir a los clientes.
3   Hay que trabajar de cara al público.
4   Debo manejar el dinero.
5   Debo ocuparme de los niños y ordenar la casa.
6   Tengo que vender bebidas, revistas y patatas fritas.
7   Hay que clasificar los documentos.
8   Hay que responder a llamadas telefónicas.
9   Debo preparar los bocadillos, el té y el café.
10 Tengo que gestionar las reservas.
11 Hay que trabajar en el ordenador.
12 Debo ayudar a los niños con sus deberes.

⚙ ACTIVITY: When do you work? – ¿Cuándo Trabajas?

Listen to the people on the audio track talking about when they work and note down:

1   the days that they work
2   the hours they do
3   how much they earn per hour
4   how they get to work

If you need to, read the transcripts below:

a   Trabajo los lunes por la tarde y los miércoles por la noche. Trabajo ocho horas por semana y gano cinco euros y ochenta céntimos por hora. Voy al trabajo en autobús y en tren.

b   Trabajo los sábados de nueve de la mañana hasta las cinco de la tarde y los domingos desde las doce del mediodía hasta las cuatro de la tarde. Trabajo doce horas por semana y gano seis euros y treinta y cinco céntimos por hora. Voy al trabajo en coche.

c   Trabajo los jueves después de clase y los viernes por la noche. Trabajo seis horas por semana y gano siete euros y quince céntimos por hora. Voy al trabajo en bici.

d   Trabajo dos veces por semana: el domingo por la mañana y el martes por la tarde. Trabajo cinco horas por semana y gano seis euros y noventa y cinco céntimos por hora. Voy al trabajo andando.

ONLINE

Head online and check out the links to help you write a CV and cover letter/email in Spanish at www.brightredbooks.net/N5Spanish

ONLINE TEST ✓

Test how well you have learned about part-time jobs at www.brightredbooks.net/N5Spanish

OPINIONS OF PART-TIME JOBS – OPINIONES SOBRE LOS TRABAJOS A TIEMPO PARCIAL

Now that you have learned how to say where you work, what job you do, what tasks you do at work, when you work, how much you earn and how you get to work, you should try to give your opinion of your part-time job. It is not enough to say that you like or dislike your job; you must give reasons for your opinions.

You can start with:

- Me encanta mi trabajo a tiempo parcial porque ...
- Me gusta mi trabajo porque ...
- No me gusta mi trabajo porque ...
- Odio/detesto mi trabajo porque ...

Then add the adjective to describe your job (if you don't know the meanings of these adjectives, use your dictionary to look them up):

... es ...

interesante	divertido	aburrido	horrible
genial	fácil	inútil	cansado
fantástico	variado	difícil	

... está ...

bien/mal pagado

THINGS TO DO AND THINK ABOUT

This is a chance for you to revise basic vocabulary such as days of the week, time phrases and numbers. Try drawing a mind map and brainstorming as much vocabulary as possible under these headings:

- days of the week
- months of the year
- time phrases (every month, week, fortnight, sometimes, often, rarely, etc.)
- numbers.

PART-TIME JOBS – LOS TRABAJOS A TIEMPO PARCIAL 3

These are very basic opinions and reasons so let's learn some fancier phrases.

DON'T FORGET

Refer to the section on describing family members on pages 8-9 if you want to describe your boss or colleagues.

ONLINE

Have a look at www. brightredbooks.net/ N5Spanish for more about part-time jobs.

 ACTIVITY: Opinions – Opiniones

Match the Spanish to the English phrases and then decide if the opinion is positive or negative. Try to make links to English words to work out what the phrases mean. If there is still language you don't understand, use your dictionary to look up the meaning.

Los clientes son simpáticos	My boss is patient and helps me
Me encanta trabajar en equipo	I have the chance to learn things
Puedo conocer a gente nueva	The customers are rude and impatient
Mis compañeros son insoportables	I don't have time to study
Tengo muchas cosas que hacer	Times passes quickly at work
Estoy muy ocupado	My colleagues are annoying
No tengo tiempo para estudiar	I love having responsibility
Puedo ganar dinero para financiar mis estudios	I have to wear a uniform and it is not comfortable
Puedo adquirir experiencia	The customers are nice
Me encanta tener responsabilidad	My boss is very strict
Tengo la ocasión de aprender cosas	The hours are very long
Nunca me aburro	I have a lot of things to do
Mi jefe es paciente y me ayuda	I can meet new people
Mi jefe es muy estricto	I love working in a team
Los clientes son groseros e impacientes	I don't have enough free time
No tengo suficiente tiempo libre	I have to work alone, and that is boring
El tiempo pasa rápido en el trabajo	I never get bored
Tengo que levantarme temprano	I'm very busy
Tengo que llevar uniforme y no es cómodo	I have to get up early
Son muchas horas de trabajo	I can gain experience
Debo trabajar solo y eso es aburrido	I can earn money to pay for my studies

 ACTIVITY

Translate the following paragraphs into English. This is good training if you choose to progress to Higher Spanish. If there are sections you are unsure of, try to focus on picking out the main points from the texts. Use a dictionary to look up any unfamiliar vocabulary.

1   Soy camarera en una cafetería del centro de la ciudad. Tengo que preparar el té y el café y servir a los clientes. Trabajo tres veces por semana y gano cinco euros y setenta céntimos por hora. Me encanta mi trabajo porque es fácil y entretenido. Siempre estoy muy ocupada y por eso el tiempo pasa rápido. Además, mi jefe es paciente y mis compañeros son serviciales. No me aburro nunca, lo cual ¡es genial!

contd

2 Trabajo como vendedor en una tienda de ropa. Debo atender a los clientes, ordenar la tienda y manejar el dinero. Lo que más me gusta es que recibo descuentos y los clientes son educados. Sin embargo, a veces detesto mi trabajo porque mi jefe es muy estricto e impaciente. Además, tengo que trabajar cuatro veces a la semana, así que no tengo tiempo libre. Finalmente, mi trabajo a tiempo parcial está mal pagado, solo gano cinco euros y veinte céntimos por hora.

3 Soy recepcionista en un hotel al lado del mar. Debo responder al teléfono, resolver los problemas de los clientes y hacer las reservas. Trabajo todos los sábados y hago nueve horas a la semana. Está bien pagado, porque gano siete euros y cuarenta céntimos por hora. Es genial porque también me dan buenos consejos. Mi jefe es muy simpático y mis compañeros son amables.

ACTIVITY: Studying and working – Estudiar y trabajar

If you go to college or university you might decide to find a part-time job to help subsidise your studies. There are advantages and disadvantages of having a part-time job at the same time as studying. Listen to the audio track to hear two people talking about having a part-time job and studying. Can you note down any advantages and disadvantages they mention?

ONLINE TEST

Test how well you have learned about part-time jobs at www.brightredbooks.net/N5Spanish

THINGS TO DO AND THINK ABOUT

Write a paragraph about your part-time job. Use the language you have learned in this section to help you. Try to include the following:

- where you work
- how much you earn
- any advantages or disadvantages there may be to having a part-time job and studying at the same time
- what you do
- how you get to work
- when you work
- your opinion of your part-time job how many hours you work
- reasons for your opinion

If you don't have a part-time job here are some sentences to help you out:

Actualmente no tengo un trabajo porque no tengo mucho tiempo disponible.

No tengo mucha experiencia laboral pero soy una persona entusiasta y que aprende rápido.

Estoy bastante concentrado(a) en mis estudios.

Aunque no tengo mucha experiencia laboral, tengo experiencia
– en el cuidado de niños
– con las nuevas tecnologías
– con los deportes

WORK EXPERIENCE – EXPERIENCIA LABORAL

In this section you will learn to describe any work experience you have done. This section will also give you the opportunity to revise the perfect and imperfect tenses, which are both used to describe actions completed in the past.

Let's start by thinking of where you might have done your work experience. Can you think of any other examples?

ACTIVITY: My work experience – Mi experiencia laboral

Read the following texts about work experiences and complete the table below.

Try to make links to English to work out what any unfamiliar vocabulary means. Use your dictionary to look up other unfamiliar language.

Mariana

Trabajé en una tienda de deportes como vendedora. Empezaba a las ocho y media y terminaba a las seis. Debía atender a los clientes y también trabajaba en la caja. Me gustó mucho el contacto con el público. Sin embargo no me gustaba el jefe porque era desagradable. En mi opinión, ese trabajo fue una buena experiencia porque era variado.

Estefanía

Durante mis prácticas de empresa, trabajé en un restaurante de comida rápida. Empezaba a las diez de la mañana y terminaba a las siete de la tarde. Tenía que preparar las patatas fritas y las hamburguesas. Lo que más me gustaba era el trabajo en equipo. Por el contrario, la jornada era muy larga y al terminar estaba muy cansada. Pienso que fue una mala experiencia porque era muy monótono.

	Where did they work?	When did they start?	When did they finish?	What did they do?	What did they like?	What did they not like?	Overall opinion
Mariana							
Estefanía							

DON'T FORGET

In your writing, try to use conjunctions such as *sin embargo*, to help structure your writing. Can you think of any more?

THE PRETERITE – PRETÉRITO PERFECTO SIMPLE

Look at the reading activity text again. You will notice that each person's work experience is being discussed in the past tense. Two tenses are being used, the preterite (*preterito perfecto simple*) and the imperfect (*pretérito imperfecto*). To revise the imperfect tense refer to page 47.

This is a great opportunity to revise when the preterite is used and how it is formed:
- The preterite is used to describe a past completed action.
- We use it with time expressions such as: *ayer, anoche, el otro día, el mes/año/verano pasado, la semana pasada, hace cinco años …*

> **EXAMPLE**
>
> Compré mi primera bici hace cinco años; Anoche cené a las diez.

1 Write down the infinitive: *hablar, vivir*
2 Now chop off the *-ar, -er* or *-ir* and add the preterite endings to the infinitive:

Subject	-*ar* verb endings	-*er* verb/-*ir* verb endings
yo	-é	-í
tú	-aste	-iste
él/ella/usted	-ó	-ió
nosotros/nosotras	-amos	-imos
vosotros/vosotras	-asteis	-isteis
ellos/ellas/ustedes	-aron	-ieron

Note

The *nosotros* forms for -*ar* and -*ir* verbs are the same in both preterite and present tense: *hablamos, vivimos.*

> **EXAMPLE**
>
> Hablamos ayer. Hablamos todos los días.

Some of the irregular verbs in the preterite tense are:

> **EXAMPLE**
>
> jugué – I played, comimos – we ate

	ser	ir	tener	hacer	dar
yo	fui	fui	tuve	hice	di
tú	fuiste	fuiste	tuviste	hiciste	diste
él /ella, usted	fue	fue	tuvo	hizo	dio
nosotros/nosotras	fuimos	fuimos	tuvimos	hicimos	dimos
vosotros/vosotras	fuisteis	fuisteis	tuvisteis	hicisteis	disteis
ellos/ellas, ustedes	fueron	fueron	tuvieron	hicieron	dieron

THINGS TO DO AND THINK ABOUT

To practise the preterite, try to complete these sentences:
- Hace unos meses, dos amigos míos _____ como camareros en un restaurante italiano. (trabajar)
- El año pasado, yo _____ a Italia de vacaciones con mis padres. (ir)
- Una vez, en una fiesta de cumpleaños, ¡me _____ ocho trozos de tarta! (comer)
- Mi hermano _____ un cuadro muy bonito hace dos semanas. (pintar)
- Hace un mes, mis primos de Australia _____ a hacernos una visita. (venir)
- Él no _____ aceptar ese contrato la semana pasada, por las malas condiciones de trabajo. (querer)
- Ayer, mi amiga y yo _____ a dar un paseo por el parque. (salir)
- Tú no _____ sobre la película que nosotros _____ el otro día. (decir/ver)

ONLINE

Learn more about the preterite and complete a further activity at www.brightredbooks.net/N5Spanish

DON'T FORGET

Let's revise **subject pronouns:**

yo	I
tú	you (informal singular)
él	he
ella	she
usted	you (formal singular)
nosotros/nosotras	we
vosotros/vosotras	you (informal plural)
ellos/ellas	they
ustedes	you (formal plural)

*In Spanish we don't always need to write the subject of an action as the verb also indicates the person who is doing it.

DON'T FORGET

The verbs *ser* and *ir* have identical conjugations in the preterite tense, you will need to know the context of the sentence in order to know which one to use. Example:
– El año pasado, mi hermano <u>fue</u> a España a trabajar allí. (Last year my brother <u>went</u> to Spain to work there.)
– Trabajar en España <u>fue</u> muy interesante para él. (Working in Spain <u>was</u> very interesting for him.)

ONLINE TEST

Take the test 'Work experience – Experiencia laboral' at www.brightredbooks.net/N5Spanish

WORK EXPERIENCE ACTIVITIES – ACTIVIDADES REALIZADAS DURANTE LAS PRÁCTICAS LABORALES

⚙ ACTIVITY: Positive or negative? – ¿Positivo o negativo?

Have a look at the following phrases and decide if they are describing something positive or negative about work experience:

1   Tenía que llevar uniforme y era cómodo.
2   Había que estar de pie durante largos períodos de tiempo, eso era cansado.
3   Pasaba horas trabajando en el ordenador, lo cual era bastante monótono.
4   Trabajaba fuera y era genial.
5   Trabajaba de cara al público, eso era interesante.
6   Trabajaba en equipo, lo que era entretenido.
7   Trabajaba solo y eso era horrible.
8   Realicé mis prácticas en el sector comercio, lo cual fue una experiencia estimulante.
9   Trabajé en el sector turismo y fue fantástico.
10 Era responsable en la caja, eso era muy entretenido.
11 No aprendí nada, fue una pérdida de tiempo.
12 Aprendí a enviar un fax, lo que fue bastante útil.

⚙ ACTIVITY: Who is it? – ¿Quién es?

Listen to the passages about work experience placements on the audio track and match the person to the statements below as best as you can. Read the statements first and pick out key words that you think will come up in the text. Listen to the text as many times as you need to in order to match all the statements.

1   I worked in a music shop.
2   I had to wear a uniform.
3   I learned some new things.
4   I worked with children.
5   I went to work by bus.
6   I met nice people.
7   I did not work in the evenings.
8   I learned how to operate a till.
9   I went to work by train.
10 I worked at the weekends.

ACTIVITY: Revision – Revisión

Read about Lucía's work experience and answer the questions which follow. Look at how many marks each question is worth and make sure that you write enough information to be awarded full marks.

Lucía

Realicé mis prácticas laborales en un colegio de primaria. Iba en autobús y después tenía que ir andando. El viaje duraba treinta minutos en total. Empezaba el trabajo a las nueve menos cuarto y terminaba a las tres y diez de la tarde. Tenía un descanso de quince minutos a las diez y media y el descanso para tomar el almuerzo era a la una. Me encargaba de ayudar a los niños a leer en pequeños grupos, de organizar juegos y de ayudar a los alumnos a hacer sus deberes. También ayudaba a los profesores a ordenar las clases y debía clasificar sus archivos. Aprendí a comunicarme bastante bien con los niños y a organizar actividades. Me lo pasé muy bien porque los niños eran realmente divertidos y estaban llenos de vida. En mi opinión, mi experiencia fue útil y variada. De hecho, en el futuro me gustaría ser maestra.

 ONLINE

For more information about work experience, head to www.brightredbooks.net/N5Spanish

Questions

1 Where did Lucía do her work experience? (1)
2 How did she get to her placement? (2)
3 How long did the journey take? (3)
4 What time did she start work? (1)
5 What time did she finish? (1)
6 When were her breaks? (2)
7 What was she responsible for? (3)
8 What did she learn? (2)
9 Did she enjoy the placement? Why? (3)
10 What has she decided to do as a result of her placement? (1)

THINGS TO DO AND THINK ABOUT

Now it is your turn to write about your work experience using the vocabulary from each of the activities in this section. Refer to the section on writing on page 82 as well to help you.

To be successful in this task, include all the information listed below and check the accuracy of your tenses using the previous activities and any other support materials you have. Make sure that your work makes sense: can you translate every word or have you left any words out? Avoid translating directly from English and use your dictionary to check the gender of nouns as well as your spelling and accents.

- Where did you do your work experience?
- How did you get there?
- What time did you start and finish?
- What did you do? Did you learn anything?
- What did you enjoy and why?
- Is there anything you didn't enjoy?
- What is your overall opinion of your work experience?

 ONLINE TEST

Take the 'Work experience' test online at www.brightredbooks.net/N5Spanish to see how well you know this topic.

MY FUTURE PLANS – MIS PLANES PARA EL FUTURO

We touched briefly on future plans when we looked at the qualities and skills needed for different jobs. Now we are going to go into more depth. Can you think of what we could cover in this section?

DON'T FORGET

There are two ways of expressing future plans in Spanish:

– by using the **near future tense**: *Ir* (conjugated) *a* + infinitive, such as: *voy a comprar un coche nuevo* (when we refer to the near future)

– by using the simple future tense: Infinitive (without -*ar*, -*er* or -*ir*) + future endings, such as: *compraré una casa nueva* (when we refer to a more distant future).

Mis planes para el futuro

- Tomarse un año sabático
- Trabajar en el sector comercio
- Continuar mis estudios
- Viajar alrededor del mundo
- Ganar dinero
- Encontrar un trabajo

USEFUL VOCABULARY

Here is some useful vocabulary to start you off. Look up any words you don't understand in the dictionary. You should listen to how these phrases are pronounced on the audio track.

Time phrases

- Más adelante
- En el futuro
- Cuando sea mayor
- Después del instituto/de la universidad

Planes de futuro

- Me gustaría ser bombero(a).
- Me gustaría trabajar como veterinario(a).
- Me gustaría trabajar en el sector comercio.
- Me gustaría ser enfermero(a).
- Me gustaría trabajar con animales.
- Quiero trabajar en el turismo.
- Quiero trabajar con los niños.
- Tengo la intención de trabajar de cara al público.
- Seré peluquero(a).
- Iré a la universidad para estudiar ciencias.
- Estudiaré formación profesional en mecánica.
- Estudiaré un curso de electricista.

DON'T FORGET

Me gustaría ser profesor means 'I would like to be a teacher': in Spanish we don't need the indefinite article *un(a)*.

ACTIVITY: My ideal job – Mi trabajo ideal

Listen to the audio track to hear three people talking about their future plans. Note down as much information as you can about the following:

1 What job do they want to do?
2 Why? (try to give at least four details)
3 What training or qualifications are they going to get?

contd

Grammar

Once you have completed the listening and read through the transcript online at www.brightredbooks.net/N5Spanish. Is there any vocabulary that you don't know and you need to look up in the dictionary? Have a look at the following phrases taken from the transcript:

- Me gustaría ser
- Iré a la universidad
- Podría conocer a nuevas personas
- Tendré la ocasión de

- Ganaré
- Seré
- Me gustaría ser
- Eso sería genial

Can you remember what the two tenses above are called? Refer to page 16 to revise the conditional, which tells you what someone *would do*, and refer to page 29 to revise the simple future tense, which tells you what someone *will do*.

 ACTIVITY: My future plans – Mis planes para el futuro

Once you have revised these tenses, complete the following sentences, putting the verb in brackets into the simple future tense. Then translate the sentences into English.

1. (Yo) _____ de cara al público, quizás en una tienda, porque me encanta el contacto con otras personas. (trabajar)
2. (Yo) _____ cocinero en un gran restaurante. (ser)
3. (Yo) quiero tratar con pacientes porque me _____ la oportunidad de ayudar a diferentes personas. (dar)
4. (Yo) _____ para una gran empresa multinacional, quizás en el sector de la informática. (trabajar)
5. (Yo) _____ un trabajo creativo, porque me encanta el diseño. (tener)
6. Todavía no sé qué _____ en el futuro, pero sé que _____ en el extranjero. (hacer/vivir)
7. (Yo) _____ un trabajo con el que _____ alrededor del mundo. (buscar/viajar)
8. (Yo) _____ un módulo de tecnología de formación profesional. (estudiar)
9. Si apruebo mis exámenes, _____ a la universidad y _____ mis estudios. (ir/continuar)
10. (Yo) _____ jugador de baloncesto profesional y _____ mucho dinero. (ser/ganar)

DON'T FORGET

Verbs like *tener* and *hacer* have irregular stems in the simple future tense and the conditional tense. Look at the verb tables in your dictionary if you can't remember their irregular forms.

 ACTIVITY: What would you do? – ¿Qué harías?

Now try the same activity but change the verbs into the conditional tense (refer back to page 16 for more on the conditional tense).

VIDEO LINK

Check out the clip 'Future work and aspirations – photography' at www.brightredbooks.net/N5Spanish

 THINGS TO DO AND THINK ABOUT

Now it's your turn. Write about your future plans and do your best to cover the following bullet points. Use the language in this section to help you, but personalise the phrases so they are relevant to you. Don't forget that you can learn this and you may wish to use it for your Performance and your writing in the Course assessment.

- What job do you want to do in the future?
- Where would you like to work/live?
- Why do you think you are suitable for this job?
- Why do you want to do this job?
- What training/qualifications do you need for this job?

ONLINE TEST

Take the 'future plans' test online to see how well you know this topic at www.brightredbooks.net/N5Spanish

CULTURE

HOLIDAYS – LAS VACACIONES 1

DON'T FORGET

You may also wish to talk about your best holiday/trip as part of your Performance.

REVISION – REVISIÓN

In this section you will learn how to describe your best holiday/trip and give your opinions on travelling. This section is a great way to revise your past tenses (both perfect and imperfect) – you should refer to pages 47 and 69 as well as the vocabulary and phrases you have already learned when revising.

Let's start by brainstorming all the vocabulary and phrases you know about holidays.

WHEN – CUÁNDO

You could refer to when your holiday is/was in a number of ways:

- En verano/en invierno/en otoño/en primavera
- En Navidad

- El año pasado
- El mes pasado
- Durante las vacaciones de verano

WHERE – DÓNDE

- A España/Francia/Alemania/Portugal ...
- A los Estados Unidos/Países Bajos/ Emiratos Árabes ...
- A Barcelona/París/Londres ...

- Al extranjero
- Al campo/a la costa/a la montaña
- A un pueblo/una gran ciudad

WITH WHOM – CON QUIÉN

You could go on holiday with a variety of different people. For example:

- Con mi familia
- Con mi amigo(a)
- Con mis amigos(as)

- Con mi clase
- Yo solo(a)

VIDEO LINK

The clip 'Booking a hotel room' will also give you some extra vocabulary: www.brightredbooks.net/ N5Spanish

FOR HOW LONG – POR CUÁNTO TIEMPO

You'll need to consider how long your trip lasted:

- Quince días
- Dos semanas

- Una semana
- Tres meses

⚙ ACTIVITY: How long was your holiday? – ¿Cuánto duraron tus vacaciones?

Thinking about the length of your trip, try translating the following sentences:

- El verano pasado fui quince días con mis amigos a Barcelona, en España.
- Durante las vacaciones de verano fui con mi familia a un pueblo al lado del mar en España.
- En Navidad pasé dos semanas en un pequeño pueblo de México, con mi madre.
- Hace tres años fui yo solo a la montaña, en Suiza, durante un mes.

Now it's your turn, write a sentence about your best holiday trip.

⚙ ACTIVITY: Accomodation – El alojamiento

Choosing from the list below, write in the facilities you could find in the following places.

alojamiento – accommodation	instalaciones – facilities
En un hotel	
En un albergue juvenil	
En un camping	
En una casa rural	
En casa de unos familiares	
En casa de unos amigos	

Using this vocabulary write about the accommodation on your holiday. Start with *Me alojé/nos alojamos en ...*

⚙ ACTIVITY: Leisure activities – Las actividades de ocio

Here are a few activities you may do on holiday. Check that you understand the meaning of each phrase. You will have many more ideas, so just add them to this list.

Ir a la playa/piscina

Ir a la discoteca

Ir al cine

Ir al museo

Ir al parque de atracciones

Practicar vela

Practicar natación

Hacer deporte

Practicar esquí

Leer una novela

Escuchar música

Visitar los alrededores

Comer en un restaurante

Comprar regalos de recuerdo

Pasear

Bañarse en el mar/la piscina

Tomar el sol

THINGS TO DO AND THINK ABOUT

The activities above are in the infinitive to allow you to change them to the imperfect or perfect tense, depending on what you want to say. Try writing five sentences about a holiday you have had and what activities you did there.

 ONLINE TEST

Test yourself on holidays online at www.brightredbooks.net/N5Spanish

HOLIDAYS – LAS VACACIONES 2

VIDEO LINK

Check out the clip 'Holidays at a summer camp' at www.brightredbooks.net/N5Spanish

REMEMBER:

- The preterite is used for completed actions in the past, for example: *El año pasado fuimos de vacaciones a la playa.*

- The imperfect tense is used for regular actions in the past/interrupted actions and descriptions, for example: *Todos los días íbamos a restaurantes a probar la comida típica española.*

ADDING INTEREST

To make this section more interesting and not just one long list of activities, you may wish to use the following expressions:

- Aprovechaba los días para (+ infinitive) – I used to spend the days + -ing (verb)

- Cuando llovía nosotros/yo (+ imperfect) – when it rained we/I used to …

- Cuando hacía buen tiempo nosotros/yo (+ imperfect) – when it was nice we/I used to …

- Todos los días nosotros/yo (imperfect) – everyday we/I used to…

- Un día nosotros/yo (+ preterite) – one day we/I + past tense

- Una vez nosotros/yo (+ preterite) – once, we/I + past tense

⚙ ACTIVITY: Grammar/Translation activity – Ejercicio de gramática/traducción

Look at the following three paragraphs. Fill in the gaps by translating the verb into Spanish and deciding whether you will use the preterite or the imperfect, or keep the infinitive.

DON'T FORGET

In Spanish we have some verbs that describe the action of a sport, such as *nadar* (to swim), *esquiar* (to ski), *patinar* (to skate).

Verónica

El año pasado, en invierno, _____ (*to go*) a Francia con mis padres. Todos los días _____ (*to ski*) en los Alpes y por la noche, _____ (*to go*) a cenar a restaurantes para _____ (*to try*) la comida típica. Un día _____ (*to go*) al pueblo más cercano para _____ (*to buy*) algunos regalos de recuerdo para la familia y los amigos.

Óscar

Hace tres años _____ (*to go*) a España con mis amigos. Todas las mañanas _____ (*to go*) a la playa o nos _____ (*to stay*) al lado de la piscina para _____ (*to suntbathe*). _____ (*to spend*) las noches en la discoteca porque nos _____ (*to love to dance*).

Rosa

Durante las vacaciones de verano _____ (*to go*) a Italia con mi madre. Los días que hacía bueno _____ (*to go for a walk*) por el centro del pueblo, _____ (*to visit*) los alrededores y _____ (*to have*) una bebida en la terraza de alguna cafetería. Un día _____ (*to go*) a Roma para _____ (*to visit*) algunos monumentos.

ACTIVITY: Opinion of the trip – Opinión sobre el viaje

You will always have an opinion of your trip. Decide if the following expressions are positive or negative and put them under the headings *opinión positiva* or *opinión negativa*.

- Fue genial
- Fue interesante
- Fue divertido
- Recomendaría este tipo de viaje
- La gente era muy acogedora
- La comida era deliciosa
- La comida no estaba muy buena
- El personal era muy servicial
- Yo no volvería allí

- Llovía todos los días
- Me divertí mucho
- La gente era muy maleducada
- Fue aburrido
- La gente no era amable
- Estaba sucio(a)
- La gente era muy simpática

DON'T FORGET

We use *fue* if we are saying how something was, for example: *el espectáculo fue muy divertido*. In the past, we use *era* for a permanent condition, and *estaba* for a temporary condition. For example: *La gente de allí era muy amable. Aguel verano, la gente estaba muy contenta con los turistas.*

ACTIVITY: The importance of travelling – La importancia de viajar

You could also add why you think travel is important.

In groups try to think, in Spanish, of ways of saying that you like to travel and reasons why. Listen to the audio track and match the parts of the sentences:

Saying you love to travel	Reasons
Me encanta viajar porque ...	... puedes descubrir nuevas culturas y tradiciones.
Me gusta ir al extranjero porque ...	... ver cómo viven otras personas.
Me gusta ir de vacaciones porque ...	... de descubrir otros países y aprender otros idiomas.
Me gusta visitar países extranjeros porque ...	... puedes hacer nuevos amigos.
Es importante viajar para ...	... te relajas y olvidas la rutina diaria.
En mi opinión, viajar es un buen medio ...	... puedes aprovechar el buen tiempo.

Now try to translate them into English.

VIDEO LINK

Watch the interview with a hotel owner at www.brightredbooks. net/N5Spanish for more vocabulary.

DON'T FORGET

When writing about a past event make sure you:
- Use the preterite and imperfect correctly
- Add some opinions
- Always check your written accuracy.

ACTIVITY: César's best holiday – Las mejores vacaciones de César

Before you try to write about your best holiday, listen to César talking about his best holiday. Copy and complete the table by putting in as much information as you can.

Cúando – when	
Dónde – where	
Con quién – with whom	
Durante cuánto tiempo – for how long	
Alojamiento – accommodation	
Actividades de ocio – leisure activities	
Opinión - opinion	

ONLINE TEST

Test yourself on holidays online at www. brightredbooks.net/ N5Spanish

THINGS TO DO AND THINK ABOUT

Now it's your turn. Using all the phrases and passages above to help you, write about a past holiday you have been on. Try to cover the categories used in the table above (César's Best Holiday).

EVENTS, LITERATURE AND FILM – EVENTOS, LITERATURA Y CINE 1

As part of the National 5 course you will be discovering different traditions, cultures and special events in the countries in which Spanish is spoken. It would be impossible to cover every eventuality in this book.

This may be the perfect opportunity for you to do some individual research on an aspect of the culture of a Spanish-speaking country. You could present your findings as part of your Performance.

Here are some traditions and cultural events that you may wish to find out more about:

VIDEO LINK

Have a look at the BBC clip about a special event at www.brightredbooks.net/ N5Spanish

ACTIVITY: Traditions and special events – Las tradiciones y ocasiones especiales

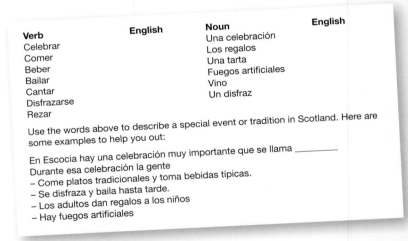

Here is some vocabulary you may wish to use when talking about traditions and special events. Try to work out what the words mean in English.

Verb	English
Celebrar	
Comer	
Beber	
Bailar	
Cantar	
Disfrazarse	
Rezar	

Noun	English
Una celebración	
Los regalos	
Una tarta	
Fuegos artificiales	
Vino	
Un disfraz	

Use the words above to describe a special event or tradition in Scotland. Here are some examples to help you out:

En Escocia hay una celebración muy importante que se llama _____
Durante esa celebración la gente
– Come platos tradicionales y toma bebidas típicas.
– Se disfraza y baila hasta tarde.
– Los adultos dan regalos a los niños
– Hay fuegos artificiales

LITERATURE AND FILM – CINE Y LITERATURA

In this section you will learn how to talk about any books you have read or films you have seen. The language used to describe books and films is very similar so we will look at both together.

Let's start by thinking about what you might like to say about a book or a film:

- What is the book/film about?
- Who are your favourite characters/actors?
- What is your opinion of the book/film?

 **ACTIVITY:** What is the book/film about? – ¿De qué trata el libro/la película?

Read the phrases below and translate them into English. You may wish to change or complete them to talk about a book you have just read or a film you have seen.

- El argumento del libro/de la película tiene lugar/sucede …
- La historia transcurre/se desarrolla en el siglo …
- El libro/la película habla de …
- El libro/la película cuenta la historia de …

ONLINE TEST

Test yourself on events, literature and film online at www.brightredbooks.net/N5Spanish

ACTIVITY: Your favourite characters – Tus personajes favoritos

Here are some adjectives which can be used to describe characters (refer back to pages 8–9 in the 'Family and friends' section for more examples).

Write out the feminine versions and English translations of these adjectives. Then use some of the adjectives to describe your favourite characters/actors.

Masculine	Feminine	English
Guapo		
Gracioso		
Malo		
Creíble		
Aburrido		
Viejo		

Mi personaje/actor favorito es/fue _____ porque (él/ella) es + adjective.

Encuentro a los personajes/actores muy creíbles, lo que hace al libro/a la película más interesante.

Los personajes del libro/de la película son/eran interesantes porque …

En mi opinión/a mi parecer/creo que el argumento es muy interesante y me gustó la relación entre los personajes.

ACTIVITY: Tus opiniones

Look at these opinions about a book/film and decide if they are positive or negative, then translate them into English.

> Me gustó mucho el libro/la película porque …

> La película me pareció un poco larga, pero me gustaron mucho los actores y la historia.

> No recomendaría ese libro/esa película porque no pasa nada interesante en él/ella.

> Me encantó esa película y en el futuro veré otras películas de ese género.

> Lo que realmente me gustó fue …

> No me gustó ese libro/esa película porque la historia era muy aburrida.

> Me decepcionó el final del libro/de la película.

> He aprendido/descubierto mucho sobre la cultura española; por ejemplo, para los españoles es muy importante pasar tiempo con la familia disfrutando de una buena comida.

> Nunca había leído/visto libros/películas de este género pero los/las recomendaría, porque la historia es verdaderamente interesante.

> Normalmente, nunca veo películas románticas/de ciencia ficción/de acción, pero esa película me gustó mucho.

> No me gustó esa película, porque no me gustan las películas de acción, son demasiado violentas.

 THINGS TO DO AND THINK ABOUT

Take some of the sentences from the activities above and write a short paragraph about your favourite book/film.

EXAMPLE

Hace una semana vi la película 'Los juegos del hambre'. Me gustó bastante, porque es muy entretenida y se parece mucho al libro. Tiene un final muy emocionante.

EVENTS, LITERATURE AND FILM – EVENTOS, LITERATURA Y CINE 2

VIDEO LINK

You may want to watch the BBC clip 'Buying tickets for a concert' at www.brightredbooks.net/N5Spanish to enhance your vocabulary.

TOP TIP

- Read each question.
- Try to find the answers in the text using the questions to help you.
- Only use your dictionary if absolutely necessary.

ACTIVITY: Opinions on a film – Opiniones sobre una película

Read the following text, in which Antonio describes a film he has just seen, and answer the questions.

Antonio opina sobre una película que acaba de ver

La semana pasada, fui al cine para ver una película británica. La película era en inglés y la historia tenía lugar en un pequeño pueblo en el sur de Inglaterra. La película cuenta la historia de cuatro amigos que no se ven desde hace 15 años y se reencuentran para pasar un fin de semana en una casa rural. Al principio, los personajes se llevan muy bien y recuerdan momentos de cuando eran jóvenes. Pero según avanza la película, empieza a haber tensión entre ellos. Al final de la película se dan cuenta de que sus vidas han cambiado y ya no tienen tanto en común. Mi personaje favorito es Luisa, porque está interpretado por una buena actriz que es muy creíble en el papel.

La película fue bastante interesante y los actores interpretaron bien su papel. Es bueno ver una película en versión original subtitulada para mejorar mi inglés.

Questions

1	When did Antonio see the film?	(1)
2	Where does the film take place?	(1)
3	What is the film about?	(1)
4	What happens:	
	a at the beginning of the film?	(1)
	b during the film?	(1)
	c at the end of the film? Give two details.	(2)
5	Why is Luisa Antonio's favourite character? Give two details.	(2)
6	What is Antonio's overall impression of the film?	(3)

Now it is your turn. Write about a film you have seen, using the vocabulary and expressions you have learned. Again you may wish to use some of this for your Performance.

ACTIVITY: Silvia's opinion on a book – La opinión de Silvia sobre un libro

Now listen to Silvia talking about a book she has just read. Complete the text below by choosing the correct word from the options below for each gap.

Silvia habla de un libro que acaba de leer

Acabo de leer un libro muy (1) _____. El argumento transcurre en (2) _____ y es una historia verídica que cuenta la experiencia de una pareja de (3) _____ británicos que se mudan a un pequeño pueblo de España. Al (4) _____ encuentran la vida un poco difícil porque no (5) _____ el idioma y echan de menos la gran ciudad. Pero al cabo de algunos (6) _____ empiezan a conocer a la gente del pueblo y (7) _____ a hablar español mejor. Mi personaje (8) _____ es Paul, el hombre de la pareja. Es muy (9) _____ y optimista porque piensa que todo va a salir bien. Al final del libro le encanta vivir en el pueblo y empieza a apreciar (10) _____ la cultura y la buena comida (11) _____. Me ha encantado el libro y lo recomendaría porque es emotivo y (12) _____ a la vez.

1 interesante/intereses

2 hace un año/2005

3 jubilados/júbilo

4 principal/principio

5 hablan/habla

6 mesas/meses

7 comienzan/comenzar

8 preferencia/preferido

9 gracioso/gracia

10 mucho/muchas

11 español/española

12 divertido/diversión

 ONLINE TEST

Test yourself on events, literature and film online at www.brightredbooks.net/N5Spanish

THINGS TO DO AND THINK ABOUT

Now you have all the vocabulary and phrases you need to describe literature and film, you may wish to start reading and/or watching films in Spanish. This is a great way to improve your language skills and also gives you an insight into the culture of Spanish-speaking countries.

Write about a book you have read using the vocabulary and expressions you have learned. Try to include:

- A brief description of the story.
- Your favourite character and why.
- Your opinion about the book.

You may wish to use some of this for your Performance.

INTRODUCTION AND BULLET POINT 1

PREPARING FOR THE WRITING EXAM

When sitting the Reading and Writing exam, you will be presented with two separate booklets:

- Reading Question and Answer booklet
- Writing Question and Answer booklet

The aim of this section is to ensure you feel fully prepared for the Writing section of the course assessment.

You will be revising some of the vocabulary and grammatical structures you have already visited in this book and will build on these to allow you to produce an accurate piece of writing that you feel comfortable with and are able to reproduce and adapt slightly on the day of your Course assessment.

The writing part of the Course assessment is worth a total of 20 marks (scaled to 15 marks) and will be 120–150 words in length. You may wish to write more, but remember that accuracy is key.

WHAT IS EXPECTED?

You will be expected to write an email in response to a job advert. The job advert will be in Spanish, advertising the job and giving other relevant details, such as the type of person they are looking for and whom to contact.

You will then have to write your email based on the four predictable bullet points (these will always be the same) and the two less predictable bullet points provided (these will change from year to year, but will always be in the context of applying for the job).

Below is an example of the job advert and the bullet points you will have to address. The first four bullet points are the predictable ones and the remaining two the less predictable ones.

> **EXAMPLE:**
>
> You are preparing an application for the job advertised below and you need to write an email in Spanish to the company.
>
> To help you to write your email, you have been given the following checklist of information to give about yourself. You must deal with all of these points:
>
> **Cafetería Central** en el centro de Barcelona busca **camarero/camarera.**
> Debes estar motivado, ser dinámico y saber hablar español e inglés.
> Para más detalles o si estás interesado/a, contacta con Sra. Gómez en la siguiente dirección de correo electrónico: Cafeteriacentral@domini.es.com
> Por favor, adjunta tu CV y responde por email, incluyendo los siguientes datos:
>
> - personal details (name, age, where you live)
> - school/college education experience until now
> - skills/interests you have which make you right for the job
> - related work experience
> - when you will be available for interview and to work
> - any links to Spain or another Spanish-speaking country.
>
> Use all of the above to help you write the email in Spanish, which should be 120–150 words in length. You may use a Spanish dictionary.
>
> As you will be talking about yourself in this email, it is important to go back and revise present tense verbs, especially the big four (*tener, ser, ir, hacer*) and the endings.
>
> We will tackle each bullet point in turn.

BULLET POINT 1: PERSONAL DETAILS (NAME, AGE, WHERE YOU LIVE)

This should be a very straightforward start, as you will have seen and used these phrases in many other contexts. However, you must know how to spell these sentences.

 ACTIVITY: Test yourself – Ponte a prueba

Choose the correct phrase from the following.

Name
se llama …   me llamo …   mi apellidos …   me apellido …   mi apellido eres …

Age
soy 16 años   tiene 16 años   tengo 16 años

Birthday
mi fecha de nacimiento es en 1990 en mayo el doce
mi fecha de nacimiento es el doce de mayo de 1990
mi fecha de nacimiento es el mayo del doce del 1990

Where you live
vivís …   vivo …   vives …
de Ayr en Escocia   en Glasgow para Escocia   en Inverness, en Escocia

How did you do? It is really important that you get off to a good start and ensure your basic Spanish is accurate.

This first bullet point does not allow for a lot of extra Spanish, although you may wish to write more about where you live. (Refer back to the section on town compared to country in the Society chapter (pages 44–7) for a recap of relevant vocabulary.)

Look at the following examples and translate them into English.

Some words have been underlined so that you can adapt the passage to suit your needs.

> **EXAMPLE**
>
> Hola, me llamo <u>Thomas</u> y tengo <u>16</u> años, mi fecha de nacimiento es el <u>16 de octubre de 1990.</u> Vivo en <u>Thurso</u>, en el <u>noreste</u> de Escocia. <u>Thurso</u> es un <u>pequeño pueblo al lado del mar</u> y tiene cerca de <u>10.000</u> habitantes.

> **EXAMPLE**
>
> Me llamo <u>Julia</u>, mi apellido es <u>Brown</u>. Tengo <u>15</u> años pero cumplo <u>16</u> años dentro de <u>dos semanas</u>. Vivo en un <u>pequeño pueblo</u> que se encuentra a <u>20 minutos de Glasgow y a 30 minutos de Edimburgo</u>, la capital de Escocia.

> **EXAMPLE**
>
> Hola, me llamo <u>Christina</u> y cumpliré <u>19</u> años el <u>12 de septiembre</u>. En este momento, vivo en <u>Perth</u>, que se encuentra en el centro de Escocia, pero soy de <u>Polonia</u>. Vivo en Escocia desde hace <u>10 años</u> y me encanta este país porque el paisaje es maravilloso.

 THINGS TO DO AND THINK ABOUT

Now it's your turn. Write a short paragraph on the first bullet point, including:

- your name
- your age
- where you live.

 DON'T FORGET

If you are struggling with some of the words, speak to your teacher/lecturer to see if you could make any changes.

 VIDEO LINK

Watch the clip 'Personal introductions' at www.brightredbooks.net/N5Spanish

 ONLINE TEST

Test yourself on this online at www.brightredbooks.net/N5Spanish

BULLET POINT 2: SCHOOL/COLLEGE EDUCATION EXPERIENCE UNTIL NOW 1

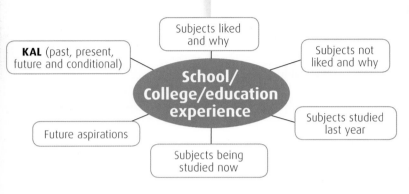

WHAT TO INCLUDE

This bullet point is about your education experience until now. If you have already studied the Learning context, then you will already be familiar with a lot of the vocabulary and grammatical structures required to complete this bullet point.

Looking at the spider diagram, it makes sense to start with a brief description of the school/college you are attending.

USEFUL PHRASES

Here are some useful phrases you could use:

Soy alumno de ...
Este año estoy en cuarto y estudio seis asignaturas.
Voy al instituto/a la universidad, donde preparo los exámenes que haré a finales de mayo.
Estudio un módulo de formación profesional de ...
Como tengo exámenes este año, aprovecho el tiempo para estudiar.

SUBJECT NAMES

Looking at the spider diagram, four of the points mention your subjects, so it is really important that you know these and their gender.

Las asignaturas

Idiomas – Languages
inglés   español   alemán   francés   italiano
urdu   gaélico   polaco   ruso   chino

Ciencias – Sciences
física   química   biología   ciencias ambientales

Artes expresivas – Expressive arts
arte dramático   arte y diseño   música   baile

Salud y bienestar – Health and wellbeing
economía doméstica   educación física

Matemáticas – Mathematics
matemáticas

Religión y ética – Religious and moral education
estudios religiosos, morales y filosóficos

Estudios sociales – Social sciences
economía   geografía   geología   historia   turismo   política

Tecnología – Technologies
informática   trabajos manuales   tecnología   comunicación gráfica

DON'T FORGET

Keep your dictionary handy while going through these phrases and make sure you understand their meanings.

SUBJECTS STUDIED LAST YEAR BEING STUDIED NOW

To show the marker you can use detailed language, try not to list all the subjects you did last year and all the subjects you are doing this year. Here are some ways you could avoid this:

El año pasado estudié seis asignaturas, incluyendo (+ two subjects).

Este año he decidido estudiar (+ subjects) a nivel de Nacional 4/5/ Higher.

El año pasado estudié ocho asignaturas, incluyendo (+ three subjects), pero este año solo estudio (+ subjects).

SUBJECTS YOU LIKED/DIDN'T LIKE AND WHY/WHY NOT

Again this should already be quite familiar to you, but it is always good to recap, so here are some expressions you could use to give your opinions and talk about subjects you like/dislike:

Opinions

Creo que ...   Pienso que ...   En mi opinión ...

Subjects you like/dislike

Love/like	Dislike/hate
*Me encanta/encantan el/la/los/las ...	*Detesto el/la/los/las ...
*Me gusta/gustan el/la/los/las ...	*No me gusta/gustan el/la/los/las ...
La asignatura que más me gusta es ...	La asignatura que menos me gusta es ...
Mis asignaturas favoritas son ...	Las asignaturas que más odio son ...

*With these expressions we need to put the **definite article** in front of the noun.

THINGS TO DO AND THINK ABOUT

Let's look more closely at what we could say about the subjects we like/dislike.

Put the phrases below under the headings *positivo* or *negativo*.

*Se me da bien el/la ...   *Se me dan bien los/las ...

*No se me da bien el/la ...   *No se me dan bien los/las ...

*En mi opinión el/la ... es útil.   *En mi opinión los/las ... son útiles.

*El/la ... me parece muy fácil.   *Los/las ... me parecen muy fáciles.

Siempre tengo buenas notas en ...

He decidido estudiar ... porque lo/la/los/las necesito para mi futura carrera profesional.

Pienso que el profesor es gracioso y no nos pone demasiados deberes.

En mi opinión es muy importante estudiar ... porque ...

Creo que el profesor es demasiado estricto y no nos ayuda con las actividades.

Elegí ... porque es una asignatura que me interesa.

*En mi opinión el/la/los/las ... es/son una pérdida de tiempo.

*With these expressions we also need to use the definite article in front of the noun.

VIDEO LINK

Check out the 'School day in Spain' clip at www. brightredbooks.net/ N5Spanish

BULLET POINT 2: SCHOOL/COLLEGE EDUCATION EXPERIENCE UNTIL NOW 2

FUTURE ASPIRATIONS

The second bullet point is probably the best place to add what you would like to do in the future.

Quick reminder

To say what you will do, or would like to do, later on in life, you will have to use the future or conditional tense. Here is a quick reminder:

Future	**Conditional**
Take the infinitive	Take the infinitive
Add endings: *-é, -ás, -á, -emos, -éis, -án*	Add endings: *-ía, -ías, -ía, -íamos, -íais, -ían*
Some exceptions:	Some exceptions:
hacer – haré	*hacer – haría*
saber – sabré	*saber – sabría*
querer – querré	*querer – querría*
decir – diré	*decir – diría*
poder – podré	*poder – podría*

Now let's look at how you can add what you would like to do in the future. It may be worth linking this to the job and/or languages.

Cuando termine el colegio me gustaría ir a la universidad para estudiar ...

En el futuro me gustaría ser ...

Después de terminar mis estudios, me encantaría tomarme un año sabático para trabajar en el extranjero/en España.

Cuando termine la universidad, me encantaría pasar un año en Madrid para mejorar mi español.

Todavía no sé qué quiero hacer cuando termine el colegio, pero algún día me gustaría vivir en el extranjero.

THINGS TO DO AND THINK ABOUT

You are now ready and armed with all the phrases you need to write your second bullet point. To help you a little more, try to complete the following passages about school using the words given in the box below. For a bigger challenge, try not to look at the words.

1. Estoy en el primer curso en el instituto Valderrama. Mi instituto es muy _____ y moderno y hay cerca de_____ profesores y 1000 alumnos. Me gusta mucho mi instituto porque tengo muchos _____ y en general me _____ muy bien con todos mis profesores. El año _____ estudié 8 asignaturas, incluyendo inglés, matemáticas y _____ . Este año _____ español, _____, francés y diseño. Me encantan las lenguas _____ porque es muy importante _____ hablar al menos dos idiomas. Por el contrario, no me gusta mucho el diseño. En mi _____, el profesor es muy _____ .

> llevo   amigos   alemán   saber
>
> cien   pasado   inglés   opinión
>
> grande   estudio   extranjeras   estricto

2. Yo soy _____ del Instituto Juan de la Cierva, donde estoy _____ mis exámenes. Mi instituto es bastante _____ pero es muy _____. Tengo una buena relación con todos mis profesores porque siempre _____ dispuestos a ayudar.

   El año _____ estudié 9 asignaturas, incluyendo matemáticas, ciencias y _____. Este _____ estudio español, matemáticas, inglés, ciencias e _____ . Mi asignatura favorita es la física. Pienso que es una _____ muy fácil y se me dan muy _____ las ciencias. Además _____ saco buenas _____ en física. Por el _____, la asignatura que menos me gusta es educación física. Me parece demasiado _____ .

> preparando   alumno   asignatura   pasado
>
> grande   música   difícil   viejo
>
> notas   historia   siempre   bien
>
> contrario   año   están

BULLET POINT 3: SKILLS/INTERESTS YOU HAVE WHICH MAKE YOU RIGHT FOR THE JOB

This bullet point allows you to write about any skills and/or interests you may have which make you the ideal candidate.

POSSIBLE WAYS OF STARTING

1 Quiero presentarme a ese puesto porque …
2 Soy la persona ideal para ese puesto porque …
3 Sería el candidato la candidata ideal porque …

These phrases could be followed with a number of different adjectives and phrases. Look at the examples below and choose the ones you feel most comfortable with to complete your sentence.

Soy …

- trabajador(a)
- amable
- creativo(a)

- muy puntual
- educado(a) y agradable siempre

- positivo(a) y optimista
- entusiasta
- serio(a)

Other personal qualities:

- Hablo español y alemán con soltura.
- Pienso que soy alguien en quien se puede confiar.
- Siempre se puede contar conmigo.

Refer to page 61 for more phrases about qualities for different jobs.

Other reasons

- Me gustaría ganar experiencia y trabajar y vivir en el extranjero.
- Me encanta visitar otros países y conocer a gente nueva.

- Me gustaría mejorar mi español y descubrir nuevas culturas.
- Me encantan los idiomas y me gustaría perfeccionar mi español.

- Estudio español desde hace cinco años y me gustaría trabajar en España para poder perfeccionarlo.

SKILLS PHRASES FOR SPECIFIC JOBS

The phrases above are very general and could be used for any job. Below are some more phrases that are suited to specific jobs.

Turismo

- Me atrae la idea de hacer una carrera relacionada con el turismo.
- Me gusta trabajar en equipo.

- Me llevo bien con todo el mundo.
- Me gusta relacionarme con el público/ los clientes.

Museo

- Me interesa el arte/la pintura/la historia.

Animador/trabajo con niños

- Me llevo bien con los niños.
- Me encantan los niños y hago de canguro con frecuencia.

- Tengo mucha energía y entusiasmo.
- Más adelante, cuando termine el instituto, me gustaría trabajar con niños.

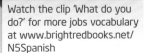

VIDEO LINK

Watch the clip 'What do you do?' for more jobs vocabulary at www.brightredbooks.net/ N5Spanish

contd

Viñedos/agricultura/camping

- Me gustaría trabajar al aire libre.
- Me gustan los animales.

INTERESTS RELEVANT TO THE JOB

This bullet point also asks you to mention any interests you may have that could make you right for the job. Really think about this: watching TV or spending time talking to your friends on Facebook etc., are probably not the interests most employers are looking for.

Again, as with bullet point 1, you will already have a lot of phrases to talk about your interests. Here are just some ideas of how to make your sentences more interesting.

Possible ways of introducing interests

- Durante mi tiempo libre, me gusta ...
- Cuando tengo tiempo libre, me gusta ...
- Si quiero relajarme, aprovecho mi tiempo libre para (+ infinitive)
- Me interesa el/la ...
- Me interesan los/las ...
- Soy un(a) apasionado(a) de ...
- Me gusta(n) mucho ...
- Mi pasatiempo favorito es ... porque ...

Sports

- Soy muy deportista y voy a correr todos los días. En mi opinión, es muy importante hacer ejercicio físico para mantenerse en forma.
- Formo parte de un club de ...
- El deporte juega un papel muy importante en mi vida.
- Cuando hace buen tiempo, me encanta practicar senderismo, montar en bicicleta o pasear.

Music

- Para descansar me gusta escuchar música.
- Me relajo escuchando música.
- Toco la guitarra/el piano desde hace ... años.
- Soy un(a) apasionado(a) de la música.

Other interests

- Me encanta el cine, sobre todo las películas extranjeras.
- Me interesa mucho la historia, por eso visito museos a menudo.
- Tengo mucha habilidad en diseño y me gusta mucho pintar y diseñar cuando tengo tiempo libre.
- Me encanta leer y por eso la lectura juega un papel muy importante en mi vida.
- Como tengo exámenes este año, paso la mayor parte de mi tiempo haciendo los deberes.

DON'T FORGET

There will be many other phrases you may wish to use, but just remember you are applying for a job, so keep it concise and relevant.

THINGS TO DO AND THINK ABOUT

A bit of a challenge now: try to translate the following sentences into Spanish. Use the phrases you have just learned to help you.

1. I would like to apply for the job, as I would like to improve my Spanish.
2. I love travelling and this job would allow me to discover a new culture.
3. I am very hardworking and I love working in a team.
4. I would be the ideal person for this job as I am polite and I get on very well with everyone.
5. When I leave school I would like to travel and work abroad.
6. In my free-time I love doing sport. I am in a hockey club and I train every weekend.
7. When I have free-time I love going for long walks with my dogs. This keeps me fit and I like being in the fresh air.
8. I am very interested in music and at the moment I am learning how to play the flute.
9. I am very passionate about art and I love to spend my time visiting art galleries.
10. When the weather is nice I like to go horse-riding in the countryside.

ONLINE TEST

Test yourself on this section online at www.brightredbooks.net/N5Spanish.

DON'T FORGET

You can revise more hobbies by flicking to the section 'El tiempo libre' (pp 22–5).

BULLET POINT 4: RELATED WORK EXPERIENCE

In this section you will be required to write about any related work experience you may have. This could be about your work experience week or a full-time/part-time job you may currently have. Refer to pages 68–71 to revise the topic of work experience.

QUICK REMINDER

Let's start with any work experience you may have done. You will need to use the preterite and imperfect tenses, so here's just a quick reminder. Refer back to pages 47 and 69 if you need more practice on these tenses.

Preterite

1. Write down the infinitive: *hablar, vivir* ...
2. Now chop off the *-ar, -er* or *-ir* and add the preterite endings to the infinitive:

Subject	*-ar* verb endings	*-er* verb/*-ir* verb endings
yo	**-é**	**-í**
tú	**-aste**	**-iste**
él/ella/usted	**-ó**	**-ió**
nosotros/nosotras	**-amos**	**-imos**
vosotros/vosotras	**-asteis**	**-isteis**
ellos/ellas/ustedes	**-aron**	**-ieron**

3. Remember to learn the irregular verbs in the preterite: *ser, ir, tener, hacer.*

Imperfect:

1. Write down the infinitive of the verb.
2. Now chop off the *-ar, -er* or *-ir* and add the imperfect endings to the infinitive:

Subject	*-ar* verb endings	*-er* verb/*-ir* verb endings
yo	**-aba**	**-ía**
tú	**-abas**	**-ías**
él/ella/usted	**-aba**	**-ía**
nosotros/nosotras	**-ábamos**	**-íamos**
vosotros/vosotras	**-ábais**	**-íais**
ellos/ellas/ustedes	**-aban**	**-ían**

3. Remember to learn the irregular verbs in the imperfect: *ser, ir, ver.*

DON'T FORGET ✚

Remember there is no article for jobs.

PAST WORK EXPERIENCE

Now we can start to write about past work experience.

Time phrases

- El año pasado
- Durante las vacaciones de verano

Where you worked

Hice unas prácticas en ... /Trabajé en ...

- un restaurante
- una oficina
- una biblioteca
- un supermercado
- una tienda de ropa
- una escuela de primaria

or

Trabajé de/como + job (remember no article before the job)

- camarero(a)
- asistente
- limpiador(a)
- cajero(a)
- vendedor(a)

ACTIVITY: What did you do? – ¿Qué hacías?

Match the Spanish phrases to the English.

Debía/Tenía que ...

preparar las mesas	look after the children	responder al teléfono	sort out the files
recoger las mesas	play with children	jugar con los niños	serve customers
clasificar documentos	set the tables	tomar los pedidos	answer the phone
servir a los clientes	welcome customers	recibir a los clientes	take orders
cuidar a los niños	clear the tables		

What you thought of it – Lo que te pareció

As you are applying for a job you may wish to make this a positive experience. Here are a few examples of some opinions you could give.

EXAMPLE

Me encantó trabajar/realizar las prácticas allí porque ...

- me sirvió como una primera experiencia en el mundo del trabajo.
- aprendí mucho.
- hice muchos amigos en un entorno distinto al del instituto /a la universidad/de la formación profesional.
- me llevaba bien con todos mis compañeros.
- fue interesante.
- ganaba mi propio dinero.

You can mix and match the reasons above, but remember to use the ones you feel most comfortable with and that you will be able to remember and reproduce accurately.

ACTIVITY: César's work experience

Listen to the audio track and answer the following questions.

1. When did César do his work placement? (1)
2. Where did he work? State any two things. (2)
3. What tasks did he have to do? Give three details. (3)
4. Why did he like the placement? State any three reasons. (3)

Now write a paragraph about any work experience and/or past job you have had.

CURRENT WORK

You may currently have a job and want to write about this. If you have a job at the moment, use the vocabulary you have just learned but with the present tense. Refer back to page 7 for this. The only real change for this part will be the time phrases:

- En este momento
- Actualmente
- Desde hace un año
- Todos los fines de semana/Todas las tardes

You are now ready to write about any job you currently have. Remember this will be in the present tense, but the vocabulary and phrases will remain the same.

THINGS TO DO AND THINK ABOUT

You should now have written the first four predictable bullet points. These bullet points will always be part of the job application and, if you learn them well, you should feel comfortable to reproduce what you have written in accurate Spanish.

DON'T FORGET

You can refer back to the employability section for more jobs.

VIDEO LINK

Check out the clip at www.brightredbooks. net/N5Spanish for more vocabulary.

DON'T FORGET

Actualmente may look like 'actually', but it is just a false friend that means 'nowadays/at the moment/ currently'.

ONLINE TEST

Test yourself online at www.brightredbooks.net/ N5Spanish

WRITING: BULLET POINTS 5 AND 6: THE UNPREDICTABLE ONES

Now let's move on to the two unpredictable bullet points. These will change every year but will still relate to applying for a job. Don't forget the contexts and topics you have already covered at National 5, as many of these could help you to complete these unpredictable points.

It would be impossible to try to cover every possibility in this book, but below are a few examples.

We will start with the examples given in the sample question paper at the beginning of this section.

WHEN WILL YOU BE AVAILABLE FOR INTERVIEW AND TO WORK?

- Estaré disponible para la entrevista el 5 de junio.
- Podría empezar a trabajar a partir del 1 de julio.

ANY LINKS TO SPAIN OR ANOTHER SPANISH-SPEAKING COUNTRY?

If you were asked to cover this bullet point you may wish to talk about a past trip to a Spanish-speaking country or maybe you visit a Spanish-speaking country on a more regular basis if you have family or friends living there.

Here are a couple of examples to give you an idea of what you could write.

EXAMPLE:

1 Hace dos años fui una semana a España. Fui con un grupo del colegio y nos alojamos en un albergue juvenil. Visitamos muchos monumentos y lugares turísticos. Me divertí mucho y mi español mejoró. Me encantaría volver.

2 Todos los años paso las vacaciones de verano en Argentina, porque mi tía vive en un pequeño pueblo no muy lejos de Buenos Aires. Paso los días paseando o bañándome en la piscina. Me encanta ir a Argentina. La comida allí es verdaderamente deliciosa, a menudo hace buen tiempo y me encanta hablar español con la gente.

OTHER POSSIBILITIES

You may be required to ask questions about something work related, therefore it is really important you know how to form a question in Spanish so you can adapt your question, no matter what it is.

Question words

What do these question words mean?

- ¿Cómo?
- ¿Quién?
- ¿Dónde?
- ¿Por qué?
- ¿Cuál/cuáles?
- ¿Qué?
- ¿Cuándo?
- ¿Cuánto tiempo?

contd

DON'T FORGET

You will have already covered this under the context of culture, so refer back to pages 74–81.

ONLINE TEST

Take the 'Unpredictable bullet points' test online at www.brightredbooks.net/N5Spanish

To form questions in Spanish you must:

- use question marks at the beginning and at the end of the sentence.
- raise your voice at the end of the question.

¿Debo llevar uniforme?

¿Están incluidos el alojamiento y la comida?

¿Tengo que trabajar los fines de semana y por la tarde/noche?

¿Tendré días de descanso?

¿Hay algún servicio de transporte desde el aeropuerto/la estación de tren hasta el lugar de trabajo?

There may be other unpredictable bullet points that have not been included here. You will be able to work on some of your own ideas with your teacher/lecturer.

You should now have a complete piece of writing.

TOP TIPS

- Always read the job advert thoroughly and apply for the job that is being advertised.
- Write in paragraphs – this will ensure you cover all the bullet points and make it easier for the marker to check your work.
- Write neatly. Markers have to mark a lot of papers and it is really important that they can read your handwriting.
- The first four bullet points will always be the same, so learn these really well.
- Learn how to spell *me llamo* and remember that in Spanish you use *tener* with your age. Get off to a good start.
- Be careful when talking about your subjects. Make sure you spell them correctly.
- Adjectival agreements – think about these carefully. They need to agree in the masculine singular, feminine singular, masculine plural and feminine plural.
- When writing a date the Spanish say, for example, *el 10 de mayo*. Do not write *10th mayo*.
- When writing about a job, do not use *un* or *una*. For example: *en este momento trabajo como camarero*, and not *trabajo como un camarero*.
- For the final two bullet points, which are less predictable, make sure your Spanish is accurate. Your teacher/lecturer will have covered many possibilities with you so try to learn these.
- Remember to always read over your work at the end. Check the following:
  - Does it make sense?
  - Have I covered all the bullet points?
  - Is my spelling accurate?
  - Have I used accents correctly?
  - Have I made adjectives agree?
  - Are my tenses accurate?
- Finally, only use the dictionary to check spelling/genders/accents. Do not try to translate phrases in your head from English to Spanish.

THINGS TO DO AND THINK ABOUT

Here are some top tips to help you learn:

- Make sure your Spanish is accurate – know your grammar points.
- To help you learn, read a line, close your jotter and write it out again.
- Check over your work.
- Make sure you fully understand what you are writing.
- Change any sentences/phrases you find difficult to remember.
- Only use a dictionary to check spelling – not to make new sentences on the day.
- Do not start learning the night before.
- Have a good revision schedule in place.
- Always check your writting.

COURSE ASSESSMENT

OVERVIEW

The Course assessment at National 5 will take the form of an Assignment (writing assssment), a Performance (talking assessment) and two question papers allowing you to demonstrate your reading, writing and listening skills in Spanish.

COMPONENT 4: ASSIGNMENT – WRITING

You will be asked to produce a piece of writing of 120–200 words in the Modern Language using detailed language based on one of the following contexts: society, learning or culture. The context of employability will be assessed in question paper 1. Throughout the year, you will prepare written pieces of work based on the topics studied which will help you to prepare for the assignment –writing.

The assignment – writing is:

- set by your centre within SQA guidelines
- conducted under a high degree of supervision and control in the classroom
- externally marked by SQA.

The assignment – writing has a total mark allocation of 20 marks, which is scaled to 15 marks.

COMPONENT 5: PERFORMANCE – TALKING

You will be assessed on at least two of these four contexts: society, learning, employability, and culture.

PERFORMANCE/TALKING (30 MARKS)

The Performance will allow you to demonstrate your ability to communicate orally in Spanish. After studying the topics at National 5, you will have prepared written pieces of work that should help you with your Performance. The Performance is made up of two parts:

- presentation – 10 marks
- conversation – 20 marks

Presentation

You will be required to give a spoken presentation in Spanish, using detailed language on a topic chosen from one of the following contexts:

- society
- learning
- employability
- culture

You will choose the topic and develop it into a short presentation of approximately 1–2 minutes to allow demonstration of your language skills, accuracy, pronunciation and intonation.

You will be allowed to refer to up to five headings of no more than eight words each as prompts during the presentation and/or use visual aids. The headings may be in Spanish or English.

You teacher/lecturer will listen to your presentation and ask questions based on it in order to engage you in a conversation on the topic.

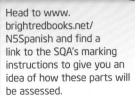

ONLINE

Head to www. brightredbooks.net/ N5Spanish and find a link to the SQA's marking instructions to give you an idea of how these parts will be assessed.

Conversation

Following the prepared presentation and any follow on questions, you will be required to take part in a conversation using detailed language on a different topic and context and to respond to some questions on that topic. The information to be exchanged will be mainly of a factual nature, but should also include some ideas and opinions. You may also ask questions where appropriate during the conversation.

Within this section marks will be awarded as follows:

- 15 marks for conversation
- 5 marks for the ability to sustain the conversation.

TOP TIPS FOR TACKLING THE EXAM

- If possible, do some practice exam papers beforehand.
- Ensure you go to bed early the night before, having done all of your revision well in advance. If you are tired on the day, it will affect your Performance.
- Ensure that your mobile phone is switched off and not kept in your pocket. If your phone goes off during the Course assessment you could be asked to leave the room.
- Make sure you have the right paper in front of you as soon as you sit down. Usually you will be given the correct one, but mistakes can be made, so don't risk it!
- Read the introduction carefully and use the questions to help lead you to the answer.
- Only use the dictionary if absolutely necessary. The first word you see in the dictionary may not be the one you need, so do read all meanings and choose the one that makes the most sense.
- Use all the time given and check your answers carefully. Remember, if they do not make sense to you, they will not make sense to the marker. Check your English too!

HOW DOES THE SQA ARRIVE AT YOUR FINAL GRADE?

Once you have completed all of your external assessments, each of the marks you achieve will be added together and you will be given an overall mark out of 100, which will translate into your grade. The percentages for achieving each grade vary, but obviously the higher, the better!

 ## THINGS TO DO AND THINK ABOUT

Now you should know:

- what is meant by the term 'Course assessment'
- what is involved in your Performance
- what is involved in the Reading/Writing paper
- what is involved in the Listening paper
- what is involved in the assignment – writing.

Be sure to make good use of this book and all of your course materials while you prepare for your National 5 assessments – you have the skills and the tools necessary to succeed and, as long as you do your best, you will achieve a grade of which you can be proud. Stay relaxed and focused and, most of all, ¡suerte!

adjectives – words that describe a noun, e.g. 'big' – *grande*; 'small' – *pequeño(a)*

adverbs – words that describe/modify verbs, adjectives and other adverbs, e.g. 'slowly' – *lentamente*; 'quickly' – *rápidamente*

comparatives – words that indicate the comparison of two or more nouns in terms of more or less, greater or lesser. We normally add 'er' to the end of an adjective or adverb to make the comparison, e.g. 'John is taller than Brian' – *John es más alto que Brian*

conditional tense –used to describe what someone would do or what would happen, e.g. 'I would play football' – *(yo) jugaría al fútbol*

conjunctions –linking words or connectors, e.g. 'and' – *y*; 'but' – *pero*; 'however' – *sin embargo*

definite article – 'the' in English; *el, la, los, las* in Spanish

false friend – a word that looks similar in two languages but means different things in each language, e.g. *sensible* in Spanish means 'sensitive' in English

imperfect tense – used to describe a past, repeated action, what used to happen, what was happening or what something was like in the past, e.g. 'I used to play/was playing football' – *(yo) jugaba al fútbol*

indefinite article – 'a' or 'an' in English, *un* or *una* in Spanish, e.g. 'I have a car' – *tengo un coche*

infinitive – the name/title/basic form of a verb that doesn't specify who is doing the verb (the subject) or when the verb is carried out (tense). In English, the infinitive has the word 'to' in front of it, e.g. 'to play'; in Spanish the infinitive will end in *-ar*, *-er* or *-ir*, e.g *jugar, comer, salir*

intensifiers – words that add force to a verb, adjective or adverb, e.g. 'really' – *realmente*, 'too' – *demasiado*

irregular past participles – verbs in their past form that do not follow the usual pattern, (e.g. in English, when the past part of the verb doesn't end in '-ed'), e.g. 'seen' – *visto*; 'done' – *hecho*

irregular verbs – verbs that don't follow a regular pattern when they are conjugated (put in different forms in different tenses), e.g. 'to have' – tener; 'to be' – ser

KAL – knowledge about language, e.g. vocabulary, grammar, tenses

modal verbs – verbs that combine with another verb to indicate mood, necessity or possibility, e.g. 'to want to' – *querer*; 'to must' – *deber*; 'to be able to' – *poder*

near future tense – used to describe what is going to happen or what someone is going to do in the near future, e.g. 'I will play football' – *(yo) voy a jugar al fútbol*

negatives – words which negate the verb, e.g. 'I don't play' – *(yo) no juego*; 'he doesn't like' – *(a él) no le gusta*; 'I never go' – *(yo) nunca voy*

nouns – words that name a person, place, thing, quality or action, e.g. 'people' – *gente*; 'classroom' – *aula*; 'pencil' – *lápiz*

past participle – to form it, in English we usually add '-ed' to the end of the verb. In Spanish, we chop off the ending of the verb and for -ar verbs, we add *–ado*, e.g. *jugado* –'played'; for *–er* and *–ir* verbs we add *–ido*, e.g. *comido* – 'finished eating'; *vivido* – 'lived'

present tense – used to describe what usually happens or what is happening in the present, e.g. 'I eat – '(yo) como'

present perfect – used to describe a recently past action, e.g. 'I have played' – *(yo) he jugado*

preterite tense – used to describe a past completed action, e.g. 'I played' – *(yo) jugué*

prepositions – words that indicate the relationship between a noun or pronoun and other words in a sentence, e.g. 'the book is on the table' – *el libro está en la mesa*

pronoun – a word that takes the place of a noun, e.g. 'John eats chocolate' can be changed to 'he eats it'

reflexive verbs – verbs that describe an action which is done to oneself, e.g. 'to wash oneself' – *lavarse*; 'I wash myself' – *(yo) me lavo*

regular verbs – verbs that follow a pattern when conjugated (put in different forms in different tenses), e.g. 'to love' – *amar*

relative pronouns – used to link what is stated in different clauses, e.g. 'who, what, which, whom, whose'. 'I have a friend who is called Marcos' – *tengo un amigo que se llama Marcos*

simple future tense – used to describe what someone will do or what will happen in the future, e.g. 'I will play football' – *(yo) jugaré al fútbol*

subject pronouns – words indicating the person or thing that does the action of the verb e.g. 'I' – *yo*; 'you' – *tú*; 'he' – *él*; 'she' – *ella*, etc.

superlatives – used in comparisons to show which noun is the most or least of a quality or characteristic, e.g. 'the tallest' – *el más grande*

tener phrases – phrases in Spanish which use the verb *tener*, e.g. *tener hambre* – 'to be hungry'

tense – indicates when the verb takes place (present/past/future)

verbs – action words, e.g. 'play' in the sentence 'I play football' – *(yo) juego al fútbol*